A GARLAND SERIES

THE ENGLISH
WORKING CLASS

A Collection of
Thirty Important Titles
That Document and Analyze
Working-Class Life before
the First World War

Edited by

STANDISH MEACHAM
University of Texas

Livelihood and Poverty

A. L. Bowley
A. R. Burnett-Hurst

Garland Publishing, Inc.
New York & London
1980

Library of Congress Cataloging in Publication Data

Bowley, Arthur Lyon, Sir, 1869– 1957.
Livelihood and poverty.

(The English working class)
Reprint of the 1915 ed. published by G. Bell, London.
1. Cost and standard of living — England.   2. Labor
and laboring classes — England.   3. England — Social
conditions — 20th century.   4. Poor — England.
I. Burnett-Hurst, Alexander Robert, 1890–   joint author.
II. Title.   III. Series: English working class.
HD7024.B7   1980   339.4'1'0942   79-56951
ISBN 0-8240-0105-2

Printed in the United States of America

THE RATAN TATA FOUNDATION
(UNIVERSITY OF LONDON)

LIVELIHOOD AND POVERTY

G. BELL AND SONS, LTD.
PORTUGAL STREET, LONDON, W.C.

NEW YORK: THE MACMILLAN CO.

BOMBAY: A. H. WHEELER AND CO.

THE RATAN TATA FOUNDATION
(UNIVERSITY OF LONDON)

LIVELIHOOD AND POVERTY

A STUDY IN THE ECONOMIC CONDITIONS OF WORKING-CLASS HOUSEHOLDS IN NORTHAMPTON, WARRINGTON, STANLEY AND READING

BY

A. L. BOWLEY, Sc.D.
READER IN STATISTICS, UNIVERSITY OF LONDON

AND

A. R. BURNETT-HURST, B.Sc.
PROFESSOR OF ECONOMICS, MUIR CENTRAL COLLEGE, ALLAHABAD ;
FORMERLY RESEARCH ASSISTANT AT THE LONDON SCHOOL OF ECONOMICS

WITH AN INTRODUCTION BY
R. H. TAWNEY, B.A.
DIRECTOR OF THE RATAN TATA FOUNDATION

LONDON
G. BELL AND SONS, LTD.
1915

THE LONDON AND NORWICH PRESS, LIMITED, LONDON AND NORWICH

THE RATAN TATA FOUNDATION

Honorary Director : PROFESSOR L. T. HOBHOUSE, M.A., D.LIT.
Honorary Secretary : PROFESSOR E. J. URWICK, M.A.
Director : MR. R. H. TAWNEY, B.A.
Secretary : MISS M. E. BULKLEY, B.Sc.

THE RATAN TATA FOUNDATION has been instituted in order to promote the study and further the knowledge of methods of preventing and relieving poverty and destitution. For the furtherance of this purpose the Foundation conducts inquiries into wages and the cost of living, methods of preventing and diminishing unemployment, measures affecting the health and well-being of workers, public and private agencies for the relief of destitution, and kindred matters. The results of its principal researches will be published in pamphlet or book form ; it will also issue occasional notes on questions of the day under the heading of " Memoranda on Problems of Poverty." In addition to these methods of publishing information, the Officers of the Foundation will, as far as is in their power, send replies to individual inquiries relating to questions of poverty and destitution, their causes, prevention and relief, whether at home or abroad. Such inquiries should be addressed to the Secretary of the Ratan Tata Foundation, School of Economics, Clare Market, Kingsway, W.C. The Officers are also prepared to supervise the work of students wishing to engage in research in connection with problems of poverty. Courses of Lectures will also be given from time to time, which will be open to the Public.

ALREADY PUBLISHED.

" *Some Notes on the Incidence of Taxation on the Working-class Family.*"
BY F. W. KOLTHAMMER, M.A. 6d.

" *The Health and Physique of School Children.*"
BY ARTHUR GREENWOOD, B.Sc. 1s.

CONTENTS

INTRODUCTION

THE last twenty years have seen the appearance of several studies of the social conditions obtaining in towns. Mr. Charles Booth's *Life and Labour in London*, which appeared in 1892, was followed in 1901 by Mr. Seebohm Rowntree's study of " Poverty " in York, and in 1907 by Mr. Howarth's and Miss Wilson's book on West Ham ; while interesting reports on Social Conditions in Dundee by the Dundee Social Union, and on Housing in Manchester and Salford by T. R. Marr, were published in 1905 and 1904 respectively. The object of the Ratan Tata Foundation in publishing the following studies of Northampton, Warrington, Stanley and Reading, is to add to the knowledge of social conditions to be derived from those works both by the investigation of new towns, and by the presentation of material as to aspects of social life which have hitherto received small attention. While, for example, the figures as to the proportions of persons living in poverty will naturally be compared with those computed by Mr. Rowntree, the tables relating to the composition of working-class households (*e.g.*, p. 29) are, it is believed, novel. It is not generally realised that the only information which we at present have as to the economic conditions of *households* is that given by the census as to the number of persons and number of rooms.

The method of inquiry, that of taking a random sample of (roughly) one in twenty working-class households, was devised by Dr. Bowley, and was first employed by him in his investigations in Reading. It is fully explained in Chapter VI. of the work, where the degree of reliability which it possesses is discussed. The results obtained by means of it are of much more than local interest, since they prove that an inquiry adequate for many purposes can be made rapidly and inexpensively by a proper system of sampling. It is to be hoped that when the simplicity of the method and the importance of the evidence which it yields are appreciated, a sufficient number of persons will be interested to make feasible the carrying out of similar investigations in other towns and in the rural districts of Great Britain.[1]

Of the chapters which follow, Chapter I. is by Dr. Bowley and Mr. A. R. Burnett-Hurst; Chapters II., III. and IV. are by Mr. A. R. Burnett-Hurst, and Chapters V. and VI. by Dr. Bowley. The enquiries at Northampton, Warrington and Stanley were conducted entirely by Mr. Burnett-Hurst, under Dr. Bowley's general supervision and detailed advice. The tabulations were carried out at the London School of Economics, with the assistance of Miss Carr, B.Litt. We are much indebted to her, and to the Royal Statistical Society for permission to reprint Dr. Bowley's paper on "Working-Class Households in Reading," which appears as Chapter V. of this volume. Those to whom we owe thanks for collecting the information contained herein are too numerous to mention individually; but we must specially express our gratitude to Mr. E. Barnes of Northampton, Mr. A. W. Perris and Mr. W. J. Rowlands of Warrington, Mr. H. James and Mr. Trevena of Stanley, and Miss S. Honey and the local branch of the Workers' Educational Association at Reading.

R. H. TAWNEY.

[1] We learn that such an investigation has been made in Bolton, of which the results will soon be available.

LIVELIHOOD AND POVERTY

CHAPTER I

(a) METHOD AND ARRANGEMENT

IN this chapter we set out in a summary form certain main conclusions obtained from enquiries conducted during the summer and autumn of 1913 into the economic conditions of three towns, the boroughs of Northampton and Warrington, and the urban district of Stanley, and from a similar enquiry carried out in Reading in the autumn of 1912. We have included also certain facts ascertained by Mr. Rowntree in the course of the enquiry which he made in 1899 into conditions of life in York, where his data appear to be comparable to those obtained by us. The method pursued in the enquiries consisted in investigating in detail a random sample of the population of the four towns, approximately one working-class house in 23 being visited at Northampton, one house in 19 at Warrington, one house in 17 at Stanley, and one house in 21 at Reading ; and it is, therefore, different from that used by Mr. Rowntree at York, where every working-class household was visited. The reader who desires to calculate from our tables the *total* number of persons in each town who fall within the different groups represented in them must, therefore, multiply our results by the appropriate number—namely 22·7 in the case of Northampton ; 19·3 in the case of Warrington ; 17·4 in the case of Stanley, and 21·5 in the case of Reading. The mathematical justification of the method of sampling, which may at first sight appear to yield unreliable results, is given in Chapter VI. of this work, where the limits within which the results can be regarded as accurate are discussed. In the present chapter only the most general results are presented. The reader will find a more detailed account of the conditions obtaining in each of the four towns in Chapters II., III., IV. and V.

The question how far the picture which we give of four towns can be regarded as representative of the conditions of urban life over the whole or the greater part of England is not easily answered. The group does not include any large city. The population of Northampton in 1911 was 90,064, of Warrington 72,100, of Reading[1] 87,693, and of Stanley 23,294. It is possible, therefore, that evidence derived from them cannot be regarded as typical of London, Liverpool, Manchester, Birmingham or Glasgow. On the other hand, it is probably not unrepresentative of the large number of towns ranging in population from 40,000 to 150,000. One feature upon which the economic character of a town very largely depends is the variety or absence of variety in its industries. Some towns are almost entirely dependent upon one staple industry and the minor industries which are subsidiary to it. Other towns have no one predominant trade, but a large number of co-existent and independent trades. Each of these types[2] is represented by two

---

[1] *i.e.*, the borough as enlarged in November, 1911.

[2] If it were so desired, it would be possible to discriminate with some precision between the two types by finding out the proportion between the number of persons employed in the main industry and in trades subsidiary to it, and the total number in any employment in the town. One could thus group the towns in varying ratios and draw a definite line where it was considered fit.

For our purpose, as the number of towns to be investigated did not exceed four, such scientific precision was unnecessary. This suggestion of a definite line of demarcation may, however,

towns among those here described. Northampton,
a boot and shoe manufacturing centre, and Stanley,
which is almost entirely dependent upon coal mining,
belong to the first type ; Warrington and Reading to
the second. Between the four towns, again, there are
very marked differences, and the type of economic experience which they represent is so various that there are
probably numerous places whose economic conditions
are at least analogous to one or other of those which were
the subjects of our enquiry. Stanley, which in several
respects (rents, housing accommodation, overcrowding,
wages and poverty) presents a marked contrast to Northampton, Warrington and Reading, offers, perhaps, a
fairly adequate picture of the conditions obtaining in a
mining village in the north of England, but supplies, of
course, both in its advantages (*e.g.*, wages) and its disadvantages (*e.g.* housing), no indication whatever of the
character of towns whose industrial environment is
different. It is, in fact, a peculiar and highly specialised
type, and the account of it is valuable by way of contrast
with centres not dependent upon coal mining as well as
by way of comparison with mining villages. Northampton
is also specialised, but not to nearly so great an extent
as Stanley ; it employs, for example, a large number of

prove of some use on a future occasion when a more extensive
series of urban studies is contemplated. Towns would then fall
into two large groups and several sub-groups, as follows :—

Group A

(*a*) Textiles—*e.g.*, Oldham, Bolton, Burnley, Huddersfield.
(*b*) Shipbuilding—Sunderland.
(*c*) Mining—Merthyr Tydvil, Annfield Plain.
(*d*) Iron and Steel—Middlesborough.
(*e*) Railways—Crewe, Swindon.
and so on.

Group B

In this group would be classed such towns as Norwich, Bristol,
etc., where there is great variety of industry.

persons engaged in the building trade. Its staple industry is one in which trade unionism is effective and wages are relatively high, though (possibly owing to the survival of a few cases of home work in the boot and shoe industry) our enquiries showed that as many as 6½ per cent. of the adult males were earning less than 18/- per week. Warrington, a town of very various industries, is remarkable for showing both a considerable group of relatively well-paid workers (38 per cent. over 30/-), and a large group of badly-paid workers (32 per cent. under 24/-). Reading has no considerable group of highly-paid workers. These two latter towns probably offer the best indication of the conditions tending to obtain in towns where a large population is engaged in unskilled labour.

The natural source with which to compare our figures as to wages is the Wage Census carried out by the Board of Trade in 1906. No summary report has as yet appeared, but the median[1] of men's earnings tabulated in the volumes hitherto published is found to be about 29/-. If the four towns are considered together, one finds that the median earnings in Warrington and Reading are below, and that the median earnings in Northampton and Stanley are above, this figure; while the median of the four towns grouped together is 26/6.[2] The difference is probably partly due to the fact that we have not extended our enquiries to any of the textile centres of Lancashire and Yorkshire, the inclusion of which might have been expected to bring up the average of the earnings both of men and of women. So far as regular workers are concerned, the earnings obtaining in London are also in all probability above the average of the earnings described in this study, though rents, of course, in London are

[1] The term median is explained on page 23, note.
[2] In the calculation Stanley is given a weight of one-quarter of the other towns, to allow for its smaller population.

exceptionally high. If, therefore, the Board of Trade's Wage Census could be taken as an entirely reliable guide, it would appear to be true to say that, while our sample accurately represents the earnings in the four towns investigated, those towns themselves, considered as a whole, are probably (as regards men's earnings) somewhat inferior to the country as a whole. The industrial north, in fact, is under-represented; the south and midlands somewhat over-represented owing to the inclusion of Reading, where earnings are abnormally low. It is possible, indeed, that the inferiority is not even so marked as our figures would at first sight suggest. For our tables include the earnings of workers in all employments, and may perhaps contain a larger proportion of casual, unskilled and specially badly-paid labour, than in the industries, principally carried on a large scale, which are included in the Wage Census.

If the information which we have obtained may be assumed to be reliable, it reveals, we think, certain facts of considerable importance. The tables in which it is summarised fall into three groups :—(1) Tables I. to IV. to show the housing conditions of the four towns investigated, Table I. giving the number of houses at each rent-group between 1s. and 13s.; Table II. classifying working-class houses according to the number of rooms contained in them ; Table III. setting out particulars as to the cases of overcrowding in each town as measured by the test explained below ; Table IV. showing the relation between rents and incomes. These tables throw light upon such questions as that of the predominant rent in each area, the predominant type of house, and the association of overcrowding with the mining industry. They also show how greatly the proportion of rent to income increases as incomes diminish.

(2) Tables V. and VI. give particulars as to the constitution of the families by which these houses are occupied,

distinguishing earners and dependants, and men, women, and children.

(3) Tables VII. to X. relate to wages and the standard of life of working-class households. Of these, Table VII. gives the earnings of adult men in the four towns investigated, together with those in York; Table VIII. the number and proportion of working-class families living above and below the poverty line as interpreted (*a*) by Mr. Rowntree, (*b*) by a new standard, together with the amounts by which household incomes exceed or fall short of it; Table IX. states the immediate causes which have depressed the condition of those families which are living below the poverty line of Mr. Rowntree; Table X. shows the number of individual persons included in the households living below the new standard, together with the proportion which each group (men, women, children) forms (i) of the total number of all persons living below the poverty line (ii) of the total number of persons (above and below the poverty line) found in the same group. From these tables, therefore, the reader is able to form a fairly reliable estimate of the proportion which families living in " primary " poverty form of all the working-class families in the four towns investigated, of the causes which depress them below the minimum standard necessary to physical health, and of the proportion of the total number of individuals living in poverty to the total working-class population. The results are, we think, surprising. In Warrington and Reading they are shocking.

The question will naturally be asked by our readers, how far the evidence presented in these pages agrees with that to be derived from a study of official reports. Where we have been able to compare the figures obtained by us with those of official publications, the correspondence is fairly close. A glance at pages 57 and 101 will show that our statistics as to the rents of working-class houses in

Northampton and Warrington conform very closely to those published by the Board of Trade (Cd. 6955 of 1913), while the description of the type of working-class house predominating in Northampton is similar. In Northampton the census report shows that the percentage of the total number of houses having more than two occupants per room (the census authorities' definition of over-crowding) is as small as ·5, while in our enquiries no houses were found with more than two occupants per room.   In Reading the official state-ment agrees almost exactly with our estimate.   In the case of Warrington, the discrepancy is somewhat greater. In that town the census report states that in more than 5 per cent. of the houses—our own report in only 3 per cent. of the houses—there are more than two persons to the room.   The difference, as explained below (p. 103), is probably due to the fact that there has been some ambiguity in the minds of the unofficial investigators as to the exact definition of a room.   The difference in the case of Stanley between the census report's figures and our own as to the proportion of houses with more than two persons per room (34 per cent. according to the census report ; 17 per cent. according to our own), is probably to be accounted for (see page 143) by the fact that since 1911 a considerable number of new houses have been erected with better accommodation.   The result of comparing our figures as to wages with information from other sources is discussed in the appropriate sections below.

We cannot compare completely the distribution of population by sex, age and number to a house with the census reports, since we have excluded from most of the detailed tables a proportion of houses which are occupied by the professional and leisured classes ; but we have not found any inconsistency indicated by the partial comparisons made.   In one important respect we obtained a nearly complete confirmation; for we compared the number of children from 5 to 14 years in each town from our sample with the number on the school registers, and found close agreement; since much of our argument rests on the number of dependent children, it is satisfactory to have this part of our evidence substantiated.

(b) RENTS AND HOUSING

We now proceed to set out the results of our enquiries in detail.   We begin with the subject of Housing.

Table I. enables a comparison to be made between the rents obtaining in different places.   The predominant rent is, it will be seen, highest in Northampton and Reading, where it is between 6/- and 7/- per week, 31 per cent. of the working-class houses being rented between those figures in the former place, and 38 per cent. in the latter.   In Warrington the largest group of houses, 44 per cent., is rented at between 4/- and 5/-.   In Stanley the largest group of rent-paying houses, 28 per cent., is rented between 5/- and 6/-, but 31 per cent. of the working-class houses in that place are let rent-free by colliery companies to workers employed in the collieries.   If these rent-free houses are left out of consideration, the town where rents are lowest is Warrington, where 16 per cent. are let at less than 4/- per week.   The town where they are highest is Reading, where 67 per cent. of the working-class houses are let at more than 6/- per week, as against 54 per cent. in Northampton, 33 per cent. in Stanley and 18 per cent. in Warrington.

Table II. shows what type of home is most commonly occupied in each of the four towns.   The six-roomed home predominates in Northampton, where 62 per cent. of the working-class houses have 6 rooms, 6 per cent. have more than 6 rooms, and 32 per cent. have less than 6

TABLE I

RENTS OF WORKING-CLASS HOUSES

RENT PER WEEK.	NORTHAMPTON.		WARRINGTON.		STANLEY.		READING.	
	Number of Houses.	Percentage.	Number of Houses.	Percentage.	Number of Houses.	Percentage.	Number of Houses.	Percentage.
Free Colliery Houses	0	0	0	0	63	30·9	0	0
1/– and under 2/–	3	·4	0	0	0	0	0	0
2/–	3	·4	11	1·7	1	·5	4	·7
3/–	52	7·5	93	14·6	6	2·9	17	2·8
4/–	85	12·2	282	44·4	4	2·0	27	4·5
5/–	173	25·0	136	21·3	57	27·9	154	25·5
6/–	213	30·7	62	9·7	53	26·0	233	38·5
7/–	107	15·4	30	4·7	10	4·9	108	17·9
8/–	35	5·0	11	1·7	3	1·5	34	5·6
9/–	12	1·7	5	·8	1	·5	12	1·9
10/–	9	1·3	5	·8	0	0	10	1·7
11/–	1	·1	1	·2	1	·5	5	·8
12/–	0	0	1	·2	0	0	1	·2
13/–	0	0	0	0	0	0	0	0
Unknown	0	0	0	0	5	2·4	0	0
Total	693	100	637	100	204	100	605	100

TABLE II

WORKING-CLASS HOUSES CLASSIFIED BY NUMBER OF ROOMS

No. of Rooms.	Northampton.		Warrington.		Stanley.		Reading.	
	Number of Houses.	Percentage.	Number of Houses.	Percentage.	Number of Houses.	Percentage.	Number of Houses.	Percentage.
1	0	0	0	0	4	2	1	·2
2	2	·3	8	1·3	39	19	4	·6
3	23	3·3	27	4·2	82	41	20	3·3
4	97	14·0	321	50·3	63	31	124	20·4
5	104	15·0	121	19·0	7	3	380	62·4
6	426	61·5	148	22·9	6	3	60	9·9
7	27	3·9	8	1·3	0	0	16	2·6
8	10	1·4	5	·8	1	·5	4	·6
9	3	·4	0	0	0	0	0	0
10	1	·1	1	·2	0	0	0	0
Unknown	0	0	0	0	1	·5	0	0
Total ..	693	100	639	100	203	100	609	100
More than two persons per room	0		19		35		9	

rooms. The five-roomed house predominates in Reading, where 62 per cent. of the working-class houses have 5 rooms, 13 per cent. have more than 5 rooms, and 24 per cent. have less than 5 rooms. The four-roomed house predominates in Warrington, where 50 per cent. of the working-class houses have 4 rooms, 44 per cent. have more than 4 rooms, and 6 per cent. less than 4 rooms. The three-roomed house predominates in Stanley, where 41 per cent. of the working-class houses have 3 rooms 38 per cent. have more than three rooms, and 21 per cent. have less than three rooms. The number of two-roomed houses (19 per cent.) in Stanley is remarkable.

TABLE III

NUMBER OF OVERCROWDED HOUSES

(FOR TEST OF OVERCROWDING, SEE BELOW)

No. of Rooms.	Northampton.	Warrington.	Stanley.	Reading.
1	0	0	4	1
2	0	3	32	0
3	2	14	32	6
4	13	67	28	27
5	14	22	2	48
6	29	18	3	2
7	2	1	0	0
8	0	1	1	0
Total overcrowded	60	126	102	84
Total No. of working-class houses	693	640	204	622
Percentage overcrowded ..	8·7	19·7	50	13·5

Table III. shows the number of cases of overcrowding revealed by our enquiries. The official definition of overcrowding is the occupation of a tenement by more than 2 persons per room. This pays no attention to the different requirements of young and old, and the detail obtained in our enquiries made a more precise measurement possible. We counted an adult (including boys over 18 and girls over 16 years) as one ; other boys and girls over 14 years as $\frac{3}{4}$; children from 5 to 14 as $\frac{1}{2}$, and children under 5 as $\frac{1}{4}$. The household is then reckoned as containing so many " equivalent adults." On this basis an average of one person or less per room is regarded as a reasonable standard of sufficiency of accommodation, and an average of more than one person per room as implying overcrowding. This definition is more stringent than that generally used.

It will be seen that on this basis, 8·7 per cent. of the working-class houses in Northampton, 19·7 per cent. of the working-class houses in Warrington, 13·5 per cent. of the working-class houses in Reading, and 50 per cent. of the working-class houses in Stanley appear to be overcrowded.[1] The figures for Stanley reveal what appears to be a very serious state of things indeed. It is little short of horrifying to discover *that one-half of all the working-class houses in that town are overcrowded.* The explanation is to be found in the peculiar circumstances which arise owing to the ownership by colliery companies of a large number (about one-third) of the houses. They grant certain houses rent-free to miners, and make certain customary allowances towards the rent of others. But if a worker is offered a rent-free house and refuses to accept it, he loses his right to the customary allowance for the rent of the house which he does take, and therefore is under a very strong inducement to occupy a rent-free house, if one is vacant, however

[1] The percentages of all occupied houses, working-class and superior, are respectively 7, 18¼, 10, and 44¼.

unsuitable, insanitary or inadequate to the size of
his family it may be. Now most of the colliery houses
are inadequate in size, for the majority of them consist
either of a kitchen and two bedrooms, or of a kitchen
and three bedrooms. Hence the existing rule as to
allowance for rent is virtually an invitation to live
under crowded conditions. Such a state of things should
certainly be brought to an end.

Table IV. shows the relation between rents and
income; column (*a*) giving the households grouped
according to their income; column (*b*) giving the median
rent[1] of the households in each income-group as a percentage of the mean income of that group. It will be seen
that the proportion which the median rent forms of the
income diminishes steadily as the income increases. It
ranges at Northampton from 44 per cent. in the case of
the lowest, to 8 per cent. in the case of the largest, income;
at Warrington from 40 to 7 per cent.; at Stanley (free
colliery houses being omitted) from 53 to 7 per cent.;
at Reading from 59 to 10½ per cent. Since, however, households whose incomes are less than 20/- are probably in an
abnormal and temporary condition, it is more interesting
to consider the groups of households whose incomes are
between 20/- and 25/-, and 25/- and 30/-, especially the
former. In the group of households whose incomes are
between 20/- and 25/-, the median rent forms 20 per cent.
of the median income at Northampton, 18 per cent. at
Warrington, 20 per cent. at Stanley, and 25 per cent.
at Reading. In the group whose incomes are between
25/- and 30/-, the median rent forms 20 per cent. of the
median income at Northampton, 16 per cent. at War-

[1] If the houses were arranged in order of rent, the median rent
would be the rent of the house half-way in this list, so that it
would have an equal number of houses above and below it. The
term " median " is used in a similar manner throughout this and
succeeding chapters.

TABLE IV

FAMILY INCOME AND RENT

Income.	Northampton. (a) No. of Households.	Northampton. (b) Median Rent[1] as Percentage of Income.	Warrington. (a) No. of Households.	Warrington. (b) Median Rent[1] as Percentage of Income.	Stanley. (a) No. of Households.	Stanley. (b) Median Rent[1] as Percentage of Income.	Stanley. No. of Free Colliery Houses.	Reading. (a) No. of Households.	Reading. (b) Median Rent[1] as Percentage of Income.
Under 10/-	20	44	14	40	4	53	0	15	59
10/- and under 15/-	14	40	5	37½	0	..	1	23	37
15 „ 20/-	24	23	11	19	1	32	0	35	30
20/- „ 25/-	44	20	111	18	2	20	2	131	25
25/- „ 30/-	72	20	96	16	8	18	4	94	22
30/- „ 35/-	132	20	74	14	17	16	8	91	19
35/- „ 40/-	77	17	71	13½	26	16	11	67	17½
40/- „ 45/-	63	15	49	11	22	13	1	47	16
45/- „ 50/-	56	14	45	11	14	11	7	28	14
50/- „ 55/-	33	13	26	10	7	11	7	18	13
55/- „ 60/-	29	10	22	9	7	9	2	11	12
60/- and over	115	8	96	7	25	7	22	26	10¼
Unknown	14	..	19	..	4	..	..	..	..
Total	693	..	639	..	137	..	..	586	..

[1] Including rates and corrected by the deduction of lodgers' payments.

rington, 18 per cent. at Stanley, and 22 per cent. at Reading.

These figures deserve attention. They show that the working-class household living on 20/- to 25/- a week spends on rent well over one-sixth of the income. *In other words, for every pound which it spends on food, clothing and other necessaries of life, it pays between 5/- and 7/- for house-room.* Since the weekly income is often, in fact, not constant through the year and the average is likely to be less than the payment for a normal week, the proportion of its annual income which it spends in rent is somewhat larger than appears from Table IV. It will be noticed, further, that in Reading, where the proportion of households living in poverty is largest, rents also are higher[1] than in Northampton or Warrington.

(c) COMPOSITION OF WORKING-CLASS FAMILIES

Of the information we have collected, at once the most accurate and the most important for many sociological purposes is that relating to the composition of families by sex, age and earning power. Hitherto there has been nothing to show how far the economic success of a household depends on subsidiary earnings, how far it is important that children should earn their own living (and even more) at the earliest age possible, to what extent unmarried women have others older or younger than themselves dependent on their earnings, how much

---

[1] The following Table compares rents for given accommodation.

Number of of Rooms.	Weekly Rents (including Rates).			
	Northampton.	Warrington.	Stanley.	Reading.
4 ..	4/3	4/3	6/3	5/6
5 ..	5/3	5/-	6/6	6/6
6 ..	6/4	6/-	9/-	7/7

pressure there is on married women to supplement
the family income, or what is the proportion of broken
families where the husband or father is dead, absent or
incapacitated. We have not completed all the interesting
analyses that could be made on such subjects, but have
given in the Appendix minute details from which investigators can obtain such information as they may want.[1]

Even more important, because it affects a larger
proportion of families, is the question as to what is the
burden which the working man has to support. It is
very common to speak of a family of man, wife and three
dependent children as normal, and minimum wage
proposals generally have this in view; and it is often
erroneously argued that the proportion of men whose
wages fall below the amount necessary for this is also
the proportion of families in poverty. We have actually
found an enormous variety of households, and our enquiry
proves that this particular grouping, though it is in some
respects the average, is itself quite rare. We cannot, of
course, follow any individual family through its economic
career, but we have some material for estimating how many
men at any one time have various responsibilities, and
to what extent the necessary minimum increases with a
man's age, and in part we can see how it is possible for
families (which have not reached or have passed their
time of stress) to help those whose difficulties are greater.
It is evident that no arrangement of payment or of work
is satisfactory that does not allow a man to develop his
earning power as he advances to maturity; if 20/- is a
satisfactory wage at 20 years, then 30/- is wanted at 30
years, and no further increase is necessary. There is,
unfortunately, no officially published information as to the
progress of wages with age, and we have not been able

[1] All the cards of the investigations are preserved at the School
of Economics for the purpose of assisting these and similar
enquiries where our published tabulation is insufficient.

to obtain much light on the subject, except in showing that the average for married men is greater than that for unmarried.

The next two tables (V. and VI.) analyse our samples of population from each of the four towns, with a view to bring out the differences and similarities between them in respect of these general characteristics. Table V. sets out individual wage-earners and dependants grouped in such a way as to reveal the number and proportion of earners and of non-earners at different ages and of different sexes. Table VI. classifies families (a) according to whether the man is or is not the sole wage-earner ; (b) according to the number of children in them.

Table V. reveals certain facts which are of considerable economic interest, to some of which we will call attention. In Northampton the proportion of wage-earners to dependants is greater than in the other three towns. This is due to the large number of women and girls who are in employment—the boot and shoe industry employs six thousand of them, while about the same number are to be found in " domestic service " and dressmaking taken together. On the other hand, though Stanley has a higher proportion of male wage-earners than either Warrington or Reading, yet it has the smallest percentage of wage-earners to the whole working-class population. There is in Stanley a lack of employment for women, and provided that there is an adult male in the house capable of earning the average wage in the district, there is little need for the women to go to work. The proportion of wives and widows at work is about 10 per cent. of all wives and widows in Northampton, 9 per cent. in Warrington, but higher—15 per cent.— in Reading. These women are chiefly charwomen, laundry workers and domestic servants in Reading, whereas in Northampton they are chiefly in the boot and shoe trade and dressmaking, since the young factory girl after marriage frequently returns to her work, though quite a considerable number are charwomen. A further point of interest arising out of the first part of this table is that in Warrington instances of children under 14 (that is of school age) at work are to be found; this is not surprising, for the reasons given, p. 107.

Turning to a consideration of the " dependants," we find that there are a larger number of men (relatively) dependent in Stanley than in the other towns. This is partly due to men being incapacitated by illness or accident when working in mines. As the Medical Officer of Health for Stanley states in his report for the year 1913, mining is " in no way an occupation directly very detrimental to the general health . . .; but indirectly one can attribute the large amount of the chronic rheumatism and likewise chest conditions in the adult population to be due entirely to their occupations ; for the workers leave the mines at all hours, and often in wet and insufficient clothing, there being a total disregard of the rigorous climate they live in."

If we merge together the 2,146 households (as to which information was sufficient) in the four towns we find that on the average there are 1·9 earners and 2·6 dependants. In more detail, per 100 households there are of wage-earners 118 men over 20 years, 26 lads and boys under 20 years, 38 females over 16 years, 6 girls under 16 ; this group is perhaps equivalent in earning power to 142 adult males. Of dependants per 100 households there are 112 males and females above 14 years, 100 children of 5 to 14 years, and 53 children under 5 years. Taking all together, one worker has to support him- or herself and 1⅓ other persons.

Table VI. shows that Stanley has the largest relative number of cases where the man is the sole wage-earner, and Northampton the smallest, of all the four towns. The percentage of cases where the male head of the family

TABLE.—EARNERS AND DEPENDANTS (INDIVIDUAL)

PRINCIPAL DIVISIONS.	NORTHAMPTON.		WARRINGTON.		STANLEY.		READING.	
	Number of Persons.	Percentage.	Number of Persons.	Percentage.	Number of Persons.	Percentage.	Number of Persons.	Percentage.
(i) Earning—								
Men over 20 ..	805	27·0	795	25·7	259	26·6	677	25·3
Lads, 18–20 ..	72	2·4	48	1·6	20	2·0	41	1·5
Others over 16 ..	121	4·0	109	3·5	34	3·5	97	3·6
,, 14–18 .. Under 14 ..	5	·2	12	·4	—	—	—	—
Total males earning	1,003	33·6	964	31·2	313	32·1	815	30·5
Women, married or widowed ..	82	2·7	48	1·6	5	·5	67	2·5
Others over 16 ..	282	9·5	164	5·3	10	1·0	158	5·9
Girls, 14–16 ..	40	1·3	45	1·4	1	·1	34	1·3
,, under 14 ..	—	—	5	·2	—	—	1	—
Total females earning	404	13·5	262	8·5	16	1·6	260	9·7
Total earners ..	1,407	47·2	1,226	39·7	329	33·7	1,075	40·2
(ii) Not Earning—								
Men over 18 ..	60	2·0	43	1·4	22	2·3	50	1·9
Lads, 14–18 ..	8	·3	4	·1	6	·6	11	·4
Women, married or widowed ..	573	19·3	589	19·1	182	18·7	449	16·8
Others over 16 ..	71	2·4	89	2·9	60	6·2	124	4·6
Girls, 14–16 ..	14	·5	12	·4	20	2·0	9	·3
Boys and girls, 5–14..	570	19·1	735	23·8	214	21·9	623	23·3
,, ,, under 5	278	9·2	391	12·7	142	14·6	334	12·5
Total not earning	1,574	52·8	1,863	60·3	646	66·3	1,600	59·8
(iii) Total earning and not earning ..	2,981	100	3,089	100	975	100	2,675	100

TABLE VI—EARNERS AND DEPENDANTS (FAMILIES)

EARNERS IN FAMILY.	NORTHAMPTON.		WARRINGTON.		STANLEY.		READING.	
	Number of Households.	Percentage.	Number of Households.	Percentage.	Number of Households.	Percentage.	Number of Households.	Percentage.
(i) Man sole earner—								
No. of children (all ages)								
0	76	11·0	62	9·7	21	10·3	65	10·6
1	71	10·2	66	10·3	38	18·7	69	11·3
2	50	7·2	57	8·9	24	11·8	58	9·5
3	34	4·9	60	9·4	21	10·3	36	5·9
4	22	3·2	32	5·0	5	2·5	23	3·7
5	6	·9	14	2·2	8	3·9	12	2·0
6 or more	8	1·2	10	1·6	3	1·5	16	2·6
Total	267	38·6	301	47·1	120	59·0	279	45·6
(ii) Man and other earners—								
No. of dependent children (all ages)								
0	155	22·4	93	14·6	13	6·4	100	16·4
1	75	10·8	56	8·8	7	3·4	42	6·9
2	68	9·8	51	7·9	15	7·4	42	6·9
3	22	3·2	35	5·5	10	4·9	36	5·9
4	25	3·4	29	4·5	6	3·0	17	2·8
5	6	·9	14	2·2	8	3·9	8	1·3
6 or more	6	·9	13	2·0	4	2·0	5	·8
Total	357	51·4	291	45·5	63	31·0	250	41·0
(iii) No man earning—								
No. of dependent children (all ages)								
0	49	7·1	27	4·2	6	3·0	60	9·8
1	13	1·9	7	1·1	3	1·5	10	1·6
2	4	·6	7	·9	4	2·0	4	·7
3	2	·3	4	·6	3	1·5	2	·3
4	1	·1	1	·2	2	1·0	5	·8
5	—	—	2	·3	1	·5	1	·2
6 or more	—	—	—	—	1	·5	0	—
Total	69	10·0	48	7·4	20	10·0	82	13·4
Grand Totals								

is assisted by wife or children is, as a result, smallest in Stanley, being only 31 per cent., whereas in Reading, Warrington and Northampton it is 41, 45 and 51 respectively.[1]

In discussions relating to minimum wages it is frequently assumed that the earnings of a grown man ought to be at least sufficient to support a wife and two children. It is obvious that for very many men, because they are unmarried, or their families are small, or their children have left school and are at work, such a standard would be unnecessarily high. So far there have been no data on which any estimate of the proportion of men who had so many dependants to all men, could be based, and it is therefore important to examine our new information on these lines.

We have in all records of 2,536 men wage-earners over twenty years. Of these, 499 (*i.e.*, 19·7 per cent.) support without assistance a wife and two or more children; thus nearly 20 per cent. of men earners have this duty. In 420 other cases (*i.e.*, 16½ per cent. in all), the household consists of a wife (with few exceptions), two or more dependent children, an adult male wage-earner, and one or more other wage-earners. We cannot in all such cases say for certain that the whole burden of support falls on one man, nor can we discriminate between the burdens on the various earners; if, then, we assume that in every case the man supports his wife and two children (and that other earners support themselves and possibly other children), we are taking the maximum possible. Thus, we obtain that certainly as many as 19·7 per cent., and not more than (19·7 + 16·5 =) 36·2 per cent. of adult male wage-earners have a wife and two or more children to support.

---

[1] It should be mentioned that the varying sizes of families in different towns cannot be deduced from this table, but only the variations in the number of dependent children.

(d) EARNINGS AND POVERTY

The question which will arouse most interest will
naturally be that of the light which these enquiries
throw upon the standard of life of the working-class
population in the four towns under consideration. We
may approach this problem in the first place by giving
a table (Table VII.), showing the normal weekly wages
of men over twenty in Northampton, Warrington, Stanley
and Reading, to which are added, for purposes of comparison, the corresponding figures[1] published for York
by Mr. Rowntree, and relating to the earnings of workers
in that city in the year 1899. By " normal weekly
wages " are meant not the wages actually earned at the
time of the enquiry, but the wages earned for a full week's
work. Unemployment and overtime have been disregarded except in the case of workers in the building
trade, where " normal weekly wages " have been calculated on the assumption that full-time is nine-tenths of the
hours worked in summer, an assumption which in all
probability somewhat underrates the loss of time caused
by unemployment through bad weather. It will be
obvious, therefore, that the figures given in Table VII.
will require considerable qualification before they can be
used to throw light upon the *actual yearly* earnings of the
workers concerned, and that merely to multiply them
by fifty-two would give a misleading and unduly opti-
mistic picture. In particular the result thus obtained
would not be comparable with that presented for York by
Mr. Rowntree in his book on *Poverty*, in which annual
earnings are calculated after additions have been made
for such items as insurance payments and income from
allotments (if any), and—a more important point—
after the loss of income incurred on account of sickness
and unemployment has been deducted. Subject to these

[1] See *Statistical Journal*, for 1902, p. 361.

TABLE VII

FULL-TIME WEEKLY WAGES OF ADULT MALES

Weekly Wage-Rate.	Approximate Percentage of Adult Males.				
	Northampton.	Warrington.	Stanley.	Reading.	York (1899).
Under 18/-	7 } 13	1·5 } 3·5	3 } 4	7 } 15	4 } 10
18/- and under 20/-	6	2	1	8	6
20/- ,, 22/-	7 } 14	15 } 28·5	2 } 5	25 } 35·5	16 } 26
22/- ,, 24/-	7	13·5	3	10·5	10
24/- ,, 26/-	9 } 24	17 } 30	2 } 16	17 } 24·5	13 } 24
26/- ,, 28/-	7	6	7	5	6
28/- ,, 30/-	8	7	7	2·5	5
30/- ,, 31/-	22 } 31	7·5 } 14·5	7 } 28	11 } 15	25 } 31
31/- ,, 35/-	9	7	21	4	6
35/- ,, 40/-	8 } 18	12·5 } 23·5	19 } 47	6 } 10	4 } 9
40/- and over ..	10	11	28	4	5
Total ..	100	100	100	100	100

c

cautions we may now set out the percentages at each of ten wage groups in the four towns and in York. In the former the workers represented are men over twenty years; in York they are men over eighteen.

Table VII. shows that the level of earnings varies very remarkably in the five towns represented in it. The proportion of relatively high earnings is largest in Stanley, as would have been expected in view of the fact that the bulk of the population of that town live by coal mining, a well-organised and comparatively well-paid trade. As against Stanley, where 75 per cent. of the workers were getting 30/- and over, 49 per cent. were getting 30/- or over in Northampton, 40 per cent. in York, 38 per cent. in Warrington, and 25 per cent. in Reading. The proportion of adult males earning 30/- and over varied, therefore, at the time of our enquiry, from three-quarters in the case of the district where earnings were highest to one-quarter in the case of the district where earnings were lowest. More striking still are the results obtained by comparing the population in the five towns earning respectively below 20/- and below 24/-. Mr. Rowntree's demonstration that so large a proportion of the adult male workers of York were earning less than 24/- a week created something like a sensation. The results of our subsequent enquiries are, we think, even more remarkable. Though, as explained above, they do not allow for sickness, unemployment and overtime, and therefore give, compared with Mr. Rowntree's figures for adult male wages, an unduly favourable picture, it will be seen from this table that, nevertheless, there were actually two towns where the proportion of workers earning less than 20/- in 1913 was larger than it was in York in 1899. While in Warrington it was 3·5 per cent., and in Stanley 4 per cent., *it was in Northampton nearly 13 per cent. and in Reading 15 per cent.* If the percentage earning less than 24/- in the different towns be compared, their order is somewhat changed. Stanley still comes first with about 9 per cent. earning below that amount, Northampton next with nearly 27 per cent., then Warrington with 32 per cent., York with 36 per cent. (in 1899), and Reading with 50·5 per cent. It will be seen, therefore, *that in four out of five of the towns more than one-quarter, and in two out of five more than one-third of the adult male workers were earning less than 24/- per week, and that (except in the case of York) irrespective[1] of the loss of earnings caused by sickness and unemployment.* In the two towns investigated by us where the proportion earning below 24/- is largest—namely Warrington and Reading—the reason is simple. In Warrington by far the largest industry is the iron trade, which employed over 7,500 male workers in 1911. In that industry there are a considerable number of men who, when working full time, earn high wages, and whose existence accounts for the fact that 23·5 per cent. of the workers in that town were earning over 35/-. But there are also a large number of labourers who for a full week of fifty-three hours received at the time of our enquiry from 20/- to 24/-, and whose minimum has since that time been fixed at 22/1 per week. In Reading the largest single employer of men's labour is a famous biscuit factory. The earnings of labourers employed by that firm cannot be stated with precision, but there is a very great proportion of unskilled work, the highest rate for which was in 1912 generally stated to be 23/- per week. Other wages for unskilled work are low, and there is no large body of skilled workers in the town to restore the average.

Important as are the figures as to the earnings of adult

[1] Irrespective also of overtime, which partially counterbalances the loss of earnings caused by unemployment.

males, they do not by themselves enable an estimate to be formed of the standard of life of the households or families included in our enquiry. The reader will, in particular, desire to know what proportion of families in each town are living in " poverty," in the sense of receiving a total income insufficient for the maintenance of physical health. Before that question can be answered it is necessary in the first place to make allowance for subsidiary sources of income, and, in the second place, to determine the line below which families can be said to be living in poverty. For a full account of the method pursued in calculating the total family income the reader may be referred to pp. 75–9. Here it is sufficient to say that all sources of income, the earnings of the wife and children, income from lodgers, from old-age pensions and other pensions are included, with the exception of charity, poor relief and subsidies (if any) from absent children. As already explained on page 32, no allowance is made for the loss of earnings caused by short time, unemployment or illness, which may be expected in most cases to outweigh overtime, and for this reason the number of households and persons falling at one time or another below the poverty line is considerably greater than appears from Tables VIII. and X. The second point, that involved in the establishment of a minimum standard, raises greater difficulties, and is discussed at length on pp. 79–83. In Table VIII. two standards have been used, of which one is that employed by Mr. Rowntree in his book *Poverty*, and the other, called throughout this book the New Standard, was worked out by us for the purpose of enquiries in Reading, but modified slightly from one town to another to meet the peculiarities of each. The differences between them are explained in detail on page 80. It should be noted that while the New Standard allows a somewhat higher minimum for an adult man and a somewhat lower minimum for a child than does

Mr. Rowntree,[1] both standards refer only to the minimum expenditure needed to maintain physical health, and make no allowance for those items of expenditure for which the ordinary man or woman will, in practice, postpone the purchase of certain " necessaries." They, therefore, share the defect of all such standards in being, to a considerable extent, abstract and arbitrary. This does not, however, destroy their utility. For though the expenditure of income may not conform to them in the case of the vast majority of families, they offer an index of the minimum income necessary to maintain physical health, provided that income is laid out with the sole purpose of maintaining it, and therefore enables one to state the *minimum* number of families whose income falls below that standard.[2] But since, in fact, expenditure very rarely is devoted to the *sole* purpose of maintaining physical health, the minimum should probably be somewhat higher than appears in this table. Further, this qualification is crossed by another. The incomes given in Table VIII. represent only incomes derived from wages, pensions and property. They do not include poor relief and charity, if any. It would not, therefore, be correct to assume that the families living in destitution are as numerous as the families stated in Table VIII. to be living in poverty. Some of them, at least, are probably obtaining some assistance from one or other of these sources. But though such assistance may cause families living below the poverty line to approximate to it more closely than is indicated in Table VIII., it may be doubted whether it raises them, except in very few cases, above it, and it may probably be neglected in considering the proportions

[1] Mr. Rowntree took the cheapest possible budget, which was largely vegetarian. The New Standard allows for some expenditure on meat and arbitrarily raises the adult male standard by 9d. a week for this purpose.

[2] Of course the expenditure on food is sometimes increased by cutting down the expenditure on rent, clothes and sundries.

living above, and the proportions living below it. With these cautions we may set out in detail the number of families in Northampton, Warrington, Stanley and Reading living respectively above and below (*a*) the minimum standard of Mr. Rowntree, (*b*) the new standard, together with the amounts by which their incomes exceed or fall short of these standards.

This table and Table IV. App. may be summarised as follows, the numbers in brackets referring to the New Standard.

In Northampton of 693 working-class families 57 (53) were below the poverty line. These are equivalent to 8·2 (7·6) per cent. of the working-class households of the town, and to 6·4 (5·9) per cent. of all households.

In addition 8 households were on, 13 possibly below, and 4 probably below the poverty line.

In Warrington of 640 working-class families 78 (74) were below the poverty line. These are equivalent to 12·2 (11·6) per cent. of the working-class households of the town, and to 11·5 (10·9) per cent. of all households. In addition 4 households were on the poverty line, 1 possibly below, and 8 probably below.

In Stanley of 203 working-class families 12 (11) were below and two were on the poverty line.

In Reading of 622 families 128 (127) were below the poverty line. These are equivalent to 20·6 (20·4) per cent. of the working-class households, and to 15·3 (15·1) per cent. of all households. Also 17 were probably and 17 possibly below the standards.

The proportion of working-class families living below either Mr. Rowntree's standard or the New Standard ranges, therefore, from (roughly) one-seventeenth in Stanley to one-twelfth in Northampton, one-eighth in Warrington, and actually just over one-fifth in Reading. It must be remembered that besides these families there

TABLE VIII

RELATION OF HOUSEHOLDS TO POVERTY LINE. PERCENTAGE OF ALL HOUSEHOLDS

	Northampton		Warrington		Stanley		Reading	
	Rowntree.	New Standard.	Rowntree.	New Standard.	Rowntree.	New Standard.	Rowntree.	New Standard.
Above Standard—								
Richer households..	22·2	22·2	5·9	5·9	10·9	10·9	24·8	24·8
Working-class households—								
Weekly excess 30/- or more	20·6	19·2	15·1	13·8	27·5	27·1	2·9	2·5
" 20/- " 30/-	18·9	16·8	12·4	12·4	19·2	17·5	5·7	4·7
" 10/- " 20/-	20·8	23·5	22·2	22·4	25·8	27·9	15·6	14·9
" 5/- " 10/-	5·9	7·1	14·0	15·1	6·1	6·6	14·0	14·6
" 4/- " 5/-	·3	··	2·5	3·2	1·3	2·2	2·7	2·3
" 3/- " 4/-	··	··	1·9	2·2	1·7	··	2·2	2·9
" 2/- " 3/-	·2	··	4·0	3·7	··	·4	3·3	3·7
" 1/- " 2/-	·2	·7	2·5	2·8	··	·4	2·5	3·4
" 0/- " 1/-	1·7	1·8	2·1	1·6	·4	·4	5·8	6·0
Amount not known	·8	·8	4·1	4·1	··	··	2·9	2·5
Total above	69·4	69·8	80·7	81·3	82·1	82·5	57·0	57·7
At Standard	·9	·9	·6	·6	·9	·9	··	··
Below Standard—								
Amount not known	··	··	··	·4	·9	·9	·7	·7
Probably below	·5	·5	·4	1·2	··	··	··	··
Weekly deficit, o/- to 1/-	·7	1·1	1·2	·9	·4	·4	·5	·7
" 1/- " 2/-	1·0	1·0	1·2	2·1	·4	··	1·9	2·7
" 2/- " 3/-	·9	·4	2·1	1·8	·9	·9	1·6	1·6
" 3/- " 4/-	1·3	1·1	1·6	1·9	·4	·4	1·8	1·9
" 4/- " 5/-	·3	·6	·9	·6	··	··	2·8	1·9
" 5/- " 10/-	1·3	1·1	3·2	2·8	1·3	1·3	5·0	4·7
" 10/- or more]	·1	··	··	·4	·9	·9	3·4	3·3
Total	6·1	5·7	12·6	12·0	5·2	4·8	17·7	17·5
Possibly below	1·5	1·5	·2	·2	··	··	··	··
Omitted	··	··	··	··	·9	·9	··	··
Total	100·0	100·0	100·0	100·0	100·0	100·0	100·0	100·0

are the actual paupers living in the workhouse and in other Poor Law Institutions.

The figures presented in Table VIII. naturally suggest two further questions. First, what are the causes which have depressed those families which are living below the minimum standards? Second, what proportion of the working-class population in each of the four towns do they include? The first question is not easy to answer, as it is obvious that more than one influence must frequently be operative, and in any case only the *immediate* causes can be stated. Provided, however, that the reader remembers that behind these immediate causes there are others of a larger and less easily defined character, we think that he will find the following table instructive.

TABLE IX

PRINCIPAL IMMEDIATE CAUSES OF POVERTY

Immediate Cause.	Percentage of households below the Rowntree Standard.				
	N.	W.	S.[1]	R.	York. 1899
Chief wage-earner dead ..	21	6	3	14	27
,, ,, ill or old	14	1	6	11	10
,, ,, out of work	—	3	—	2	3
Chief wage-earner irregularly employed	—	3	—	4	3
Chief wage-earner regularly employed :—					
Wage insufficient for 3 children :					
3 children or less ..	21	22	1	33 ⎫	
4 children or more ..	9	38	1	15 ⎬	57[2]
Wage sufficient for 3 but family more than 3 ..	35	27	1	21 ⎭	
Total	100	100	12	100	100

[1] The figures for Stanley are too small to be expressed in percentages.   [2] For further details see p. 173.

When two or more factors were operating to drag the families down, we have selected in our classification that which appeared to be the predominant factor at the time of our enquiry.

The facts expressed in this Table appear to us to be of considerable importance as revealing the principal immediate causes of " primary " poverty. It will be noticed that in all places except Stanley the principal cause is low wages. In Stanley—though the figures are too small for much weight to be laid upon them—the single largest group consists of households where the chief wage-earner is ill or old, while only 1 out of 11 households is below the poverty line because the head of the household is in regular work at low wages. The figures are to be explained by the peculiar conditions of life in a mining centre, where, on the one hand, wages are relatively high, and, on the other hand, accidents are more numerous than they are in connection with other industries. In the three other towns which we investigated, and in York, the causes which depress families below the minimum standard arrange themselves in a series different from that obtaining at Stanley. In Warrington and Reading the principal cause is the inadequacy of wages to support three children, in Northampton the inadequacy for larger families. In York there was a large proportion of cases where the chief wage-earner was dead. In no town does permanent unemployment or irregularity of work of a capable man rank as an important cause.

With Table IX. before him, the reader will not require us to emphasise the enormous part played by low wages in causing primary poverty. Actually *one-half of the households below the poverty line at Warrington and Reading, nearly one-half at York, and one-third at Northampton, were living in poverty because the wages of the head of the household were so low that he could not support a family of three children or less.* It is thus proved that a great part of the poverty revealed by our enquiries—and we have no reason to regard their results as other than representative—is not intermittent but permanent, not accidental or due to exceptional misfortune, but a regular feature of the industries of the towns concerned. It can hardly be too emphatically stated that of all the causes of primary poverty which have been brought to our notice, low wages are by far the most important. We would go further and say that to raise the wages of the worst-paid workers is the most pressing social task with which the country is confronted to-day.

The second question of importance is that of the numbers and proportion of the working-class population in each of the four towns investigated who are below the minimum standard, who are living, that is, in " primary poverty." This differs from the proportion of the households, since on the whole the poorer households are the more populous. That question is answered in Table X. It sets out (*a*) the number of persons living below the New Standard classified by age and sex ; these, being the numbers in our samples, should be multiplied by about 20 (see p. 11) to give the numbers in the towns ; (*b*) the proportion which the number in each group forms of the total number of persons living below the poverty line ; (*c*) the proportion which the number in each group below the poverty line forms of the total number in that group, thus : in Northampton 34 men earning are below the line, while Table V. (p. 29) shows that there are in all 805 men earning ; that is about 4 per cent. of this group are below the line. In the case of Stanley percentages are not given, as the number of observations is too small to allow of percentages having any significance.

An examination of this Table brings to light certain very remarkable facts. *First*, if we take the whole working class population of both sexes and all ages in each of these four towns, and ask what proportion of it is above and

TABLE X

PERSONS IN WORKING-CLASS HOUSEHOLDS BELOW THE NEW STANDARD

Persons	N.			W.			S.	R.		
	(a) No.	(b) %	(c) %	(a) No.	(b) %	(c) %	No.	(a) No.	(b) %	(c) %
I.—*Earning*										
Men ..	34	12·8	4	66	14·5	8	4	110	14·1	15·5
Women ..	19	7·1	5	16	3·5	7·5	4	43	5·5	14·5
Lads 18-20	2	·8	3	4	·9	7	1	3	·4	—
Boys 14-18	1	·4	1	8	1·8	16	2	23	2·9	25
Girls 14-16	3	1·1	7	9	1·9	20	1	8	1·0	26
Sch. children	2	·8	—	2	·4	—	0	1	·1	0
Total earning	61	22·9	4·4	105	23·1	8·5	12	188	24·0	16·5
II.—*Dependent*										
Men ..	13	4·9	22	5	1·1	12	6	16	2	32
Women ..	50	18·8	8	73	16·0	11	9	135	17·3	23·5
Lads & Boys	1	·4	—	1	·2	—	0	4	·5	—
Girls ..	2	·8	—	2	·4	17	0	1	·1	—
Sch. children	91	34·2	16	181	39·8	25	25	286	36·6	47
Infants ..	48	18·0	17	88	19·3	22·5	8	152	19·4	45
Total depend.	205	77·1	13·0	350	76·9	19	48	594	76·0	37
III.—*Total earning and dependent* ..	266	100	9	455	100	15	60	782	100	29

what proportion of it is below the minimum standard, we find that the percentage below is in the case of Northampton 9, in the case of Warrington 15, in the case of Reading 29, in the case of Stanley 60 out of 975, or 6 per cent. Put otherwise: in Northampton 1 person in every 11, in Warrington just over 1 person in every 7, in Stanley one person in every 16, *in Reading more than one person in every* 4 of the working classes, was at the time of the enquiry living in " primary poverty," and that in spite of the fact that no allowance was made for short time or

unemployment. The percentage of the whole popula-
tions, including the upper classes of each town, living in
poverty, exclusive of inmates of workhouses, etc., were
respectively about 7, 12, 4½ and 19.

Second, the proportion of persons of the working-class
living below the line is in each town greater, as would be
expected, in the case of dependants than in the case of
earners. Of the latter 4·4 per cent. in Northampton, 8·5
per cent. in Warrington, 12 out of 329 (4 per cent.) in
Stanley, 16·5 per cent. in Reading were living in " primary
poverty." Of the former 13 per cent. in Northampton,
19 per cent. in Warrington, 48 out of 646 (7·4 per cent.)
in Stanley, 37 per cent. in Reading were in a similar condition. It would appear, therefore, that it is upon the
non-wage-earning members of the working-class that the
burden of poverty falls with the most crushing effect.

Third, the preceding statement suggests that an
examination of the Table would show that of the seven
different groups (men, women, lads, boys, girls, school
children and infants) appearing in it, some groups have
a much larger proportion living below the poverty line
than others. This is, in fact, the case.

Thus the proportion of poor dependent men is sur-
prisingly large, especially in Reading, where they form 32
per cent. of all the dependent men above and below the
poverty line. But it is when one turns to the two groups,
" school children " and " infants," that one finds the
proportion living in poverty most striking. The figures
may be summarised as follows :—

Of school children who are not earning, 16 per cent. in
Northampton, 25 per cent. in Warrington, 25 out of 214,
or 12 per cent. in Stanley, and 47 per cent. in Reading,
are living in poverty.

Of infants under five years 17 per cent. in Northampton, 22·5 per cent. in Warrington, 5·5 per cent. in Stanley
and 45 per cent. in Reading are living in primary poverty.

It must, of course, be remembered that " Primary Poverty " has here a technical meaning, viz., that the actual earnings (including pensions) of the family, when pooled together, are insufficient to give all members the food and clothing of the New Standard, after paying for rent, food and household sundries. It does not necessarily follow that so large a proportion of children are actually underfed ; for school-feeding, presents, and poor relief help in some cases, and there is probably some squeezing of sundries. Further it is very probable that the mother suffers before the children. Nevertheless the standard is so low, and assumes so much thrift and knowledge, that the impression given is probably not exaggerated.

The condition of things revealed by these figures is so serious as scarcely to need comment. That in Northampton *just under one-sixth of the school children and just over one-sixth of the infants;* in Warrington *one-quarter of the school children and almost a quarter of the infants;* in Reading *nearly half the school children and 45 per cent. of the infants* should be living in households in primary poverty irrespective of exceptional distress caused by bad trade or short time, is a matter to cause the gravest alarm. The proportion of children and infants who *at one time or another* have lived or will live below the standard taken as necessary for healthy existence, must be much greater even than these large figures show. If the figures on page 40 suggest, as they do, that the primary object of social reform should be to bring about an advance in the wages of the worst-paid workers, the figures just quoted give very strong support to those who hold that it is essential in the meantime to make adequate provision for the feeding of school children[1] and the care of infants.[2]

---

[1] See *The Feeding of School Children*, by M. E. Bulkley, published for the Ratan Tata Foundation (G. Bell & Son, 3/6).

[2] See *Round about a Pound a Week*, by Mrs. Pember Reeves. (G. Bell & Son, 2/6.)

(e) CONCLUSION

If the reader who has had patience to follow what has, we fear, been a somewhat arid and forbidding exposition, will pause at the end to allow his impressions to arrange themselves in " a wise quietness," he will, we think, find the uneasiness produced by particular details of the picture intensified rather than weakened by reflection upon its general features. It is so often said that the real volume of poverty is exaggerated—it was said again and again when Mr. Rowntree's book on York was published—that those who do not come into contact with it regard the descriptions of it by those who do as the fruit of an overheated imagination, and those who do begin in time to doubt the evidence of their own eyes. Our figures show that, quite apart from the " secondary " poverty of those whose income is injudiciously spent, and quite apart from accidents—or rather certainties— such as temporary sickness and unemployment, permanent, as distinct from occasional, poverty exists in certain places on a scale which is really appalling. Let us for a moment obliterate the boundaries between the different towns which we have described, and regard them as merged into one large city. The city contains about 2,150 working-class households [1] and 9,720 persons. Of those households 293, or $13\frac{1}{2}$ per cent.—of those persons, 1,567 or 16 per cent.—are living in a condition of primary poverty. [2] It is often implied that the wages of an adult workman are normally sufficient to bring up his family in decency ; but out of 2,285 adult males in our composite city as to whose earnings we have definite information, 729 or 32 per cent. were, at the time of our enquiry, earning less

---

[1] Throughout this paragraph 480 houses inhabited by the middle and upper class are excluded.

[2] i.e. if (in a few cases) poor relief and help from absent children are not taken into account.

than 24/– a week. It is often implied that the causes which bring men into poverty are within their own control, that they are the masters of their fate and the creators of their misfortunes. In many cases this may be so ; yet the extent to which it is true is exaggerated, Of households living in poverty, the cause is to be found in the death of the chief wage-earner in 14 per cent., in his illness or age in 11 per cent., in his unemployment in 2 per cent., in the irregularity of his work in 2 per cent., in the fact that his income is insufficient for his family of three children or less in 26 per cent. of the cases, and in his inability to support his family of four children or more in 45 per cent. (in nearly half of this last group he could not support even three). It is often implied that the children of the working-classes have as good a chance as those of the well-to-do of a life of independence and health. But out of 3,287 children who appear in our tables, 879 *or* 27 *per cent. are living in families which fail to reach the low standard taken as necessary for healthy existence ;* and apart from these there are the very numerous children in Poor Law institutions who, though presumably adequately fed and clothed, are otherwise handicapped. The figures are, we venture to think, beyond all reasonable doubt, and, as we have already explained, they take no account of sickness and temporary unemployment.

There is the further even more serious consideration that since the main incidence of poverty is among families where there are three or more children below school age and no subsidiary earners, it follows that many other families have passed through this stage and only risen out of it when the children began to earn, and that another large number recently married will (if conditions do not alter) fall into poverty as the third or fourth child is born. The proportion of children, therefore, who during some part of the first fourteen years of their lives are in households of primary poverty, is considerably greater even than that found in an instantaneous survey. Facts such as these require no comment. The causes and the remedies for them do not come within the scope of this monograph.

CHAPTER II

NORTHAMPTON has achieved such prominence as an industrial and political centre that it is hardly necessary to make any introductory remarks about the town. Situated in the beautiful Nene Valley and free from the smoke and dirt which one always associates with a manufacturing town, Northampton is not readily realised to be the very centre of one of the most prosperous industries of the country. Although its inhabitants are mainly dependent upon the boot and shoe trade, other industries of considerable importance are carried on and give employment to a large number of persons. The staple industry together with its allied trades employed in 1911 about 11,900 men and boys and 6,200 women and girls, that is to say, 42 per cent. and 43 per cent. respectively of the total male and female persons occupied, after excluding professional occupations, persons engaged in Central and Local Government, and persons serving in the army. The building trade comes next in importance of men's occupations, employing 2,300 males. Of females, domestic service employed 2,900, and dress 2,500. The number of persons engaged in various occupations in 1911 are grouped under main headings in the table on the following page.

Period of Investigation

The investigation was carried out in July, 1913, a month which proved suitable for the purpose. That employment during the month of July may

PERSONS ENGAGED IN CHIEF OCCUPATIONS OF
NORTHAMPTON (1911)

Occupations	Males, 000's	Females, 000's
Central and Local Government } Defence .. .. } Professional Occupations .. }	16	8
Domestic Service	5	29
Commercial	18	5
Transport	24	..
(Railways	8)	
Agriculture : Nurserymen, etc.	7	..
Metal, Machines, etc.	20	..
Building	23	..
Woodwork	8	..
Skin, Leather, etc.	9	2
Printing, Bookbinding, etc. ..	5	6
Dress	4	25
Boot and Shoe	110	60
Food	23	10
Gas, Water, etc.	3	..
General Workers	9	2
Others	13	6
Total	297	153

be regarded as being normal is shown by the *Labour
Gazette's* monthly report upon unemployment. Information has also been obtained from official sources as to the
demand for labour during 1913 in the more important
industries of Northampton, and it indicates that, taken
as a whole, employment was about the average of the
previous years. The following is a description of the

state of trade and employment in 1913 in the chief industries of the town :—

 Building Trade.—Very good, a marked improvement on former years.

 Clothing Trade.—Good, better than usual, due to seasonal slackness in the staple, *i.e.,* " shoe " trade, enabling the firms to get sufficient female labour.

 Breweries.—Normal, though possibly more labour employed through the increase in the bottled beer trade.

The *Labour Gazette* of the Board of Trade, referring to the amount of unemployment in July in the boot and shoe trade throughout the country, states that " employment, on the whole, continued good for the time of year." It should be pointed out that the shoe trade is rather slack in July because that month is " between seasons," the busy season lasting from January to Whitsuntide. The bigger firms, however, endeavour so to regulate the production that little, if any, short time is worked. One firm which employs a very large number of operatives stated that it avoids overtime and works no short time, at least the last occasion it did so was nineteen years ago.[1] Speaking of employment in Northampton in July, 1913, the Board of Trade stated that " employment showed little change compared with a month ago (when it was stated to be generally good) ; it was fair with lasters and finishers but rather quiet with clickers and pressmen."

The amount of employment in any town constantly varies, and if any comparison is to be made between the results from different towns, it will be necessary for persons

---

[1] At times when one department gets through more work than another it has to wait till the other department " catches it up." The result of this is that in the meantime some persons are being temporarily unemployed or under-employed.

to be regarded as being in normal full-time employment, and for them to be credited with those earnings which they receive when fully employed, though at the time of the enquiry they may have been working short time. This has been done in the cases of Northampton and the other towns in all industries except building.[1]

Method of Enquiry

The method of enquiry was by examination of households selected as forming an adequate sample of the town, and thereby differed from Mr. Rowntree's York investigation, in which every working-class household was visited. The adequacy of the method is discussed in Chapter VI. The detailed working was as follows :—
The first step taken was to obtain as full a list as possible of the residents in the borough. For this purpose a local directory was utilised and in this every twentieth house or building was noted. These were next classified according to whether they were dwelling-houses, shops, or institutes, etc. In Kelly's County Directory of Northampton a list of the principal residents in the borough is given and it was assumed that persons whose names were recorded in this list did not belong to the wage-earning class and that others did. It was found that a small proportion not on this list were in the middle class, but there is every reason to believe that when these were excluded the remainder practically coincided with the wage-earning class.

The number of buildings noted was 1,020 in all. Of these it was found that 124 were shops, factories, institutions, non-residential buildings, etc., whilst 153 were found under the heading of principal residents. The remainder (743) were assumed, in the first instance, to be working-class houses. Investigators then visited each one and obtained and entered as much information

[1] See below p. 72.

as possible relating to the facts printed on the card of enquiry (see Appendix, p. 187). In a number of instances a great deal of supplementary information was entered on the back of the cards. In five cases the houses had been demolished. The investigators were instructed that, when a house was found to be empty, they were to visit the house on the left of the vacated one ; otherwise under no circumstances were they to substitute another house for that marked even in the event of information being refused.

The cards relating to these 743 houses were then scrutinised and finally tabulated. Upon examination it was found that in 45 of the 743 houses the occupiers were not members of the wage-earning class (professional men, clerks, managers, master builders, etc.), and the houses were on this account excluded from the tables relating to the wage-earning class. The results of the tabulation of the remainder, and the conclusions drawn from them, form the subject of this chapter.

The Census of Population (Vol. VI.) gives the following facts relating to the borough in April, 1911 :—

	NUMBER.	POPULATION.
Inhabited dwelling-houses and flats	17,113	79,207
Empty	547	..
Inhabited shops	1,490	6,647
Hotels, etc., offices, workshops, etc., and miscellaneous ..	302	1,617
Institutions	45	2,593
Uninhabited buildings	84	..
	19,581	90,064

The number of inhabited houses on June 1, 1913, was obtained from official sources, and was stated to be

20,112, whereas the number of tenantable houses on the same date was said to be 20,402. Hence it is probable that at the time of the enquiry there were about 20,200 inhabited houses, and in our sample there were 891 (198 principal residents and 693 other inhabited houses) ; our sample, that is to say, was 1 in 22·7. This multiplier *twenty-two and seven-tenths* [1] will have to be applied to all figures in the sample, if estimates for the whole of the borough are made.

Housing and Rents

The view of Northampton which a traveller obtains from a railway carriage indicates a flourishing town of recent growth, for he sees row upon row of modern red-brick dwellings. This is true only of the new portion of the town, and, as one would naturally expect, housing conditions in the older quarters are less favourable. Not only are the houses old, tumble-down, and in many cases unfit for habitation, but they are cramped in narrow streets and courts. In recent years there has been a movement on the part of the Borough Council to deal with these congested areas. The disappearance of the courts off Bridge Street is evidence of its activity, and already large numbers of dwellings have been demolished or condemned.[2] There are still, however, numbers of

---

[1] The reason why 22·7 and not twenty is here adopted is that the sample of one in twenty was selected from the directory which, though professing to cover the whole town, actually omits those houses where the names of persons could not be obtained. Further, a directory is soon out of date in a growing town. Hence the houses covered by the directory are a smaller number than those actually in the town at the time of the enquiry, and it is found that of these latter our sample is nearly one in twenty-three, whereas of the former we took one in twenty. The same remarks will apply to the multipliers in the other two chapters. There is no reason to think that any bias is thus introduced.

[2] Two or three years ago the number of houses assessed at £8 and under was 7,188, since then 120 of these have been condemned.

dwellings in the Castle, North and South Wards of the borough which should, and probably will, receive the attention of the local authorities before long. A detailed criticism of dwellings which should be condemned can only be made when a complete house-to-house investigation, at any rate of suspected houses, is made. With respect to housing, a sample enquiry is reliable only in relation to questions of rents, accommodation, and over-crowding.

In Table I. is given the number of households paying various rentals. The Table also shows the relationship between the number of rooms in a house and its rent, the bulk of the households pay a rent varying from 5/– to 7/9. When these are grouped in shilling classes, as in the Table, it is seen that the largest class is that with rent from 6/– to 6/9.

The largeness of the number of families living in six-roomed dwellings in Northampton should be noticed. In striking contrast to this we find that throughout the country the proportion of six-roomed houses among the wage-earning classes is low. In Northampton there are in all 426 houses out of a total of 693—that is to say three-fifths—which are six-roomed ; while half this number are four or five-roomed dwellings. It should be explained that under the term " room " the investigators were told to include only sitting-rooms, bedrooms and kitchens, and to exclude sculleries, bathrooms, passages and large cupboards.

The houses for the most part have flat fronts rising directly from the pavement, for it is only with the better class of property that one finds bay windows and small front gardens. Many houses have back yards or gardens, some of which are quite extensive. These latter are to be found, to a great extent, in Far Cotton, the rural ward of the borough. The five-roomed house which the Board of Trade in its Report on Working Class Rents and Retail

Prices in 1912 regarded as the predominant type[1] is described as follows :—

" The front door opens into a passage. On the ground floor are a parlour and a living-room or kitchen (with separate scullery), while on the first floor are three bedrooms. There is generally a fair-sized garden. Six-roomed houses, which are also common, are of the same general plan as the five-roomed, but they have an additional living-room on the ground floor and the scullery is not built over. The type of house occupied by labourers is one of four rooms and a scullery."

TABLE I

NUMBER OF WORKING-CLASS HOUSES CLASSIFIED ACCORDING TO RENTS AND ROOMS

Weekly Rent (including rates).	Number of Rooms.										Totals.
	1	2	3	4	5	6	7	8	9	10	
1/– to 1/9	..	..	3	..	..	..	..	..	..	..	3
2/– ,, 2/9	..	..	2	1	..	..	..	..	..	..	3
3/– ,, 3/9	..	2	13	33	4	..	..	..	..	..	52
4/– ,, 4/9	..	..	4	39	31	11	..	..	..	..	85
5/– ,, 5/9	..	..	..	19	36	114	3	1	..	..	173
6/– ,, 6/9	..	..	1	4	17	185	5	1	..	..	213
7/– ,, 7/9	..	..	..	1	12	84	7	2	1	..	107
8/– ,, 8/9	..	..	..	..	3	22	8	2	..	..	35
9/– ,, 9/9	..	..	..	..	..	7	3	2	..	..	12
10/– ,,10/9	..	..	..	..	1	3	1	1	2	1	9
11/– ,,11/9	..	..	..	..	..	..	..	1	..	..	1
12/–	..	..	..	..	..	..	..	..	..	..	..
Totals ..	..	2	23	97	104	426	27	10	3	1	693
Median Rents		3/–	3/6	4/3	5/3	6/4	7/6	8/1½	10/–	..	6/–

[1] It is possible that the definition of " scullery " differed in the two enquiries.

[This Table should be read as follows :—
In the sixth column (that is to say in the column relating to houses with six rooms) and in the fifth row (the row relating to houses with rents from 5/– to 5/9) is the figure 114. This means that there are 114 houses which contain six rooms, and for which the rents (inclusive of rates) are from 5/– to 5/9. The other details of the table are to be interpreted in a similar way.]

The relationship between the rent of houses and the number of rooms they contain is also shown in Table I. It is seen that a four-roomed house usually has a rent of 3/– to 5/– ; that one-third of the five-roomed houses are let at a rental of 5/– to 5/9, and for a six-roomed house the tenant has in most cases to pay from 5/– to 8/–, over 40 per cent. of these houses being rented at 6/– to 6/9.

The Board of Trade in the above-mentioned report on Working-Class Rents (Cd. 6955 of 1913) gives the predominant weekly rents in Northampton for dwellings with varying number of rooms. Below comparison is drawn between these official figures and the results of Table I.

	Four Rooms.	Five Rooms.	Six Rooms.
Board of Trade Report	4/– to 5/–	5/– to 5/9	6/6 to 7/9
Northampton Enquiry	4/– to 4/9	5/– to 5/9	6/– to 6/9

It should be noted that the Government returns refer to May, 1912, while the Northampton enquiry figures relate to July, 1913.

So far we have considered the *number* of rooms in relation to rent. But from the hygienic standpoint, the cubic contents of rooms are more to be regarded than their number, and floor space is also important, for it is this which limits sleeping accommodation. It is necessary to take into account the fact that there are great variations in the height of rooms in different towns. For this purpose measurements were made of typical houses, the results of which are given in Appendix Table I^N. (p. 188).

A point which is especially interesting is that in Northampton large numbers of houses are owned by wage-earners, special opportunities being given for them to acquire property by various building societies.[1] But this ownership of property created a difficulty which had to be faced when compiling Tables I. and VII. In the case of the former Table information was obtained as to the net rental of the house, that is to say, the rent which would have to be paid if the owner was a tenant, exclusive of rates. The rates in Northampton in 1913 were 7/7 in the £, except in the Far Cotton Ward, where they were 6/7. To this net rental were added the rates paid by the owner—the total forming the gross rental which was entered in Table I.

There is a number of houses of £20 to £50 a year to be found in Northampton, whilst houses with rentals up to £150 per annum or more are procurable, as Northampton

---

[1] It is extremely difficult to obtain reliable information relating to the number of dwellings owned by the working-men of Northampton. A society, however, which has played a great part in enabling such men to acquire property is the Northampton Town and County Benefit Building Society. At the present time it has 1,500 borrowing shareholders on its books. Most of these are working-men, some of whom are the owners of more than one house. The method adopted by the directors is to advance about two-thirds of the purchase money, the remainder being found by the person borrowing. The repayments are allowed to extend over a period of 15½ years, but can be paid off at an earlier date if desired. Many young people also invest small amounts (the minimum is 4/– a month) in the Investors' Department until they have a sum large enough to entitle them to go in for a house, the Society helping them with an advance.

is a county town where a large proportion of persons are not wage-earners.

In Table II. is given the size of the household in relation to the number of rooms. This Table is of importance, as it shows the extent of overcrowding and enables us to compare our results with those obtained by the Census officials. It should be noted, however, that no inferences as to size of family can be drawn from the Table, as lodgers and all persons living in the dwelling at the time of the enquiry are included.

TABLE II

NUMBER OF WORKING-CLASS HOUSES CLASSIFIED ACCORDING TO THE NUMBERS OF PERSONS AND OF ROOMS

No. of Rooms	Number of Persons in House.												Totals
	1	2	3	4	5	6	7	8	9	10	11	12	
1	..	..	..	..	..	..	..	..	..	..	..	..	..
2	1	1	..	..	..	..	..	..	..	..	..	..	2
3	4	6	6	5	1	**1**	..	..	..	..	..	..	23
4	1	29	22	15	15	10	3	**2**	..	..	..	..	97
5	2	11	24	15	16	18	10	5	1	**2**	..	..	104
6	7	62	87	81	77	41	34	22	10	4	..	**1**	426
7	..	3	4	7	4	2	2	1	3	..	..	1	27
8	1	..	3	3	2	..	1	..	..	..	..	..	10
9	..	1	..	..	..	1	..	1	..	..	..	..	3
10	..	..	..	1	..	..	..	..	..	..	..	..	1
Totals	16	113	146	127	115	73	50	31	14	6	..	2	693

The numbers in heavy type show the cases where there were exactly 2 persons to a room.

For the purpose of drawing comparisons with official statements the definition of overcrowding which the Census authorities use (viz., more than 2 persons to a room) has been adopted. Out of the 693 households, there are 463 (or 67 per cent.) with less than one person to a room ;

81 (or 12 per cent.) with exactly one person; 149 (or 21 per cent.) with between one and two, and *no cases of overcrowding according to the above definition.* If one turns to the Census report one finds that the tenements with more than two occupants per room number 109, or ·5 per cent. of the total number of tenements. The reason for this difference is explained in Chapter VI.

As the test used by the Census authorities may well be regarded as too lenient, a new and more elastic one has been adopted. In the new test, boys from 14 to 18, and girls from 14 to 16[1] are regarded as requiring ¾ of the space essential for an adult, and hence equivalent to ¾ of an adult. Similarly children from 5 to 14 are taken as ½ and infants (children under 5) as ¼. By this means children are expressed in fractions of adults, or, as we shall call them, " equivalent adults." These fractions being substituted for the children in each household, a Table similar to No. II., but upon the new basis, has been built up. Overcrowding is then considered to exist where there is more than one equivalent adult to a room.

It will be seen that there are 60 cases where overcrowding exists, half of these being found in six-roomed houses, while about a quarter are found in five-roomed houses;[2] that is to say, more than one-twelfth of the 693 households are overcrowded upon this basis. Also 25 in number (about 4 per cent.) have reached the standard, while the remainder have more room than required. This test is more scientific than the one adopted by the Census authorities, as it is based upon the needs of the persons. Though these standards are somewhat arbitrary, either

[1] This allows for the need for more space in houses where there were adolescents of both sexes.

[2] A five-roomed house contains from 2,500 to 3,000 ft. (see Appendix, Table I[N].). It should then accommodate 5 to 6 equivalent adults allowing 500 cu. ft. for each adult, with a little give and take. One equivalent adult or less per room may then be regarded as a reasonable standard of sufficiency.

TABLE III

NUMBER OF WORKING-CLASS HOUSES CLASSIFIED ACCORDING TO THE NUMBERS OF EQUIVALENT ADULTS AND OF ROOMS

No. of Rooms.	NUMBER OF EQUIVALENT ADULTS IN HOUSES.																	
	1	1½	1¾	2	2¼	2½	2¾	3	3¼	3½	3¾	4	4¼	4½	4¾	5	5¼	5½
1	..	..	..	..	..	..	..	..	..	..	..	..	..	..	...	..	..	..
2	1	1	..	..	..	..	..	..	..	..	..	..	..	..	..	..	..	..
3	4	7	..	..	3	2	..	5	1	1	..	..	..	..	..	..	..	..
4	1	..	2	28	5	7	6	15	5	6	4	5	2	2	2	5	1	..
5	2	..	..	11	9	6	5	14	1	4	5	9	1	7	9	7	1	2
6	7	..	..	62	19	24	16	64	18	24	11	42	18	11	16	34	8	4
7	..	..	..	3	2	1	1	1	2	1	4	1	1	..	2	..	1	1
8	1	..	..	..	1	..	..	3	..	..	2	..	..	..	1	1	..	..
9	..	..	..	1	..	..	..	..	..	..	..	..	..	..	..	..	1	..
10	..	..	..	..	..	..	..	..	..	1	..	..	..	..	..	..	..	..
Totals	16	8	2	105	39	40	28	102	27	37	26	57	22	20	30	47	12	7

No. of Rooms.	5¾	6	6¼	6½	6¾	7	7¼	7½	7¾	8	8¼	8½	8¾	9	9¼	9½	9¾	Totals.
1	..	..	..	..	..	..	..	..	..	..	..	..	..	..	..	..	..	..
2	..	..	..	..	..	..	..	..	..	..	..	..	..	..	..	..	..	2
3	..	..	..	..	..	..	..	..	..	..	..	..	..	..	..	..	..	23
4	..	1	..	..	..	..	..	..	..	..	..	..	..	..	..	..	..	97
5	3	5	1	..	..	1	..	1	..	..	..	..	..	..	..	..	..	104
6	12	7	7	4	3	5	3	1	1	2	1	..	1	..	..	..	1	426
7	..	2	1	..	..	1	..	1	..	..	..	..	..	..	..	1	..	27
8	..	..	..	1	..	..	..	..	..	..	..	..	..	..	..	..	..	10
9	..	..	..	..	..	..	..	..	..	1	..	..	..	..	..	..	..	3
10	..	..	..	..	..	..	..	..	..	..	..	..	..	..	..	..	..	1
Totals	15	15	9	5	3	7	3	3	1	3	1	..	1	..	..	1	1	693

The numbers in heavy type show the cases where there is exactly the equivalent adult per room.

test can be interpreted with the aid of the tables of cubic contents of rooms as given in the Appendix, and they serve the purpose of showing the tendency to overcrowd, if not of the extent of overcrowding in one town as compared with another.

Earners and Persons dependent upon them

In Table II[N]. (Appendix), p. 190, it is shown how these groups of wage-earners and non-wage-earners are composed according to sex and age. Very nearly half the population are earners, and thus to each earner there is on the average little more than one dependant. Of the earners 57 per cent. are men over 20 years, 14 per cent. are lads and boys under 20, 28 per cent. are women and girls, of whom three-quarters are unmarried and over 16 years. Of the dependants the great majority are wives or children under 14 ; the remainder consists of a few men ill, incapable or past work, and of a few boys and girls not yet started. There are very few unmarried persons of either sex or any age capable of work and not actually earning.

Per 100 households we find at work 116 men over 20 years old, 28 lads and boys, and 58 women or girls ; while dependent there are 84 married women, 82 school children, 40 children under five years, and 22 other persons ; in all 203 earners and 227 non-earners.

Of the 805 men and adult sons, it is found that 573 are heads of households, 25 are lodgers, 65 live with their working mother or non-working parents, and 142 work with their father or other men.

Through the kindness of the Education Officer we are enabled to give the number of school children on the Admission Registers of the Public Elementary Schools on January 31st, 1912. There were 6,586 boys and 6,490 girls between the ages of 5 and 14 years, making a total of 13,076. Of these we should have 1 in 22·7, that is, 576, or somewhat less, since we have excluded shops from the scope of our enquiry, whereas a number of shop-keepers' children attend the elementary schools. The number found is 570.

Above have been given the facts as to individuals, but information relating to families is equally, if not more, important. In the next table a classification has been adopted, which at once shows the number of children[1]

---

[1] Dependent children are in the great majority of cases under 14 years old and have not left school, but there is a small number

dependent upon each group of wage-earners. One sees at once from the Table that the most considerable group is the one where the man is the sole wage-earner. This group forms 38½ per cent. of the whole. In 224 other cases the man is assisted in maintaining the family by one or more of his children. In 7 per cent. of the families both the man and his wife are at work, while in the same number of cases women, girls and lads support the family because of the death or incapacity of the adult male.

For information as to the size of the family it is necessary to compile a further table, which can be obtained from the detailed classification of households in the Appendix (Table III^{N}.), p. 194. Though this classification is cumbersome, it gives results of no little importance, for it serves to show how great are the variations in the composition of working-class families. Statisticians have for some years adopted the practice of regarding the typical family as being composed of a man, wife and three children. There are about 330 distinct groupings in 693 households, and of the latter there are only 31 cases where the statisticians' so-called " normal family " is to be found.

Looking into Table III^{N}. (Appendix) in detail, certain salient points stand out prominently.

There are 63 cases where the children are sole earners, and in 24 of them, that is, over one-third, there is an adult male in the family who is a dependant.

Moreover, there are 24 cases where there are " no earners "—that is to say, the head of the family, and

of lads and girls who are not yet settled in a trade, and another small number of older persons who through incapacity or idleness or from domestic duties are not at work for gain. In Tables IV., p. 64, and IV. N, W, R and S (Appendix) sons and daughters of all ages are included in the term ; but in Table III. N, W, R and S (Appendix) only those under 18 years (lads) or 16 years (girls) are included. This applies to all the towns and the corresponding summaries.

TABLE IV—EARNERS AND DEPENDENT CHILDREN

Dependent Children of all Ages	Man alone earning (Number of Households)	Man and 1 or more Children earning (Number of Households)	Man and Wife earning (Number of Households)	Other cases where at least one Man over 20 years is working (Number of Households)	Women, Girls, and Lads under 20 earning (Number of Households)	No earnings (Number of Households)
0	76	86	17	52	30	19
1	71	49	13	13	12	1
2	50	42	11	15	2	2
3	34	17	2	3	1	1
4	22	22	1	2		1
5	6	4	0	2		
6	4	3	2			
7	4	1				
	267[1]	224	46[2]	87	45	24

[1] Wife is living in all cases but 5 in first group and 8 in second. Adult non-earners in first group = 16 (not counting wife). Adult non-earners in second group = 32 (not counting wife).

[2] In 11 cases one or more sons and daughters are earning, and in 5 others an additional adult is earning.

probably the wife as well, are too old to work, and are either living on their savings or receiving pensions or charity. This class also includes several spinsters and widows who take in lodgers and eke out in many cases a precarious existence.

In a very small percentage of cases (about 2 per cent.), the wage-earner works on his or her own account, that is to say, he is his own employer. The rag and bone man is probably the most obvious example of this class.

Further, with regard to the statement made in Chapter I., p. 31, concerning the assumption made in wage discussions, that an adult male has to support a wife and two or more children, we find that in Northampton at least 120 or 15 per cent. of the 805 adult male wage-earners are called upon to do this, while it is possible that a further 127 or 15½ per cent. may have to bear this burden.

Earnings and Rates of Wages

So far the information upon which the preceding Tables were based was given quite readily by most householders, though in some cases it was refused. In cases of refusal it was obtained from other reliable sources and confirmed by neighbours' statements. But over the question of earnings more difficulty was incurred. It happened that frequently the information was elicited in conversation without the householder being aware of the fact. Definite statements of the wages of married householders were made in 96 per cent. of the cases, for other men and boys in 91 per cent., and for unmarried women and girls in 94 per cent. It was found, as one would naturally expect, that in the poorest quarters persons were very willing to give the required information, and were anxious, in fact, to tell the life history of the family. Also, though in some families the head of the household would refuse to state his wage, yet he was quite ready to state those of his children. In those cases where the wife stated

B

her husband's wage the investigators were cautioned not to accept it as the husband's actual wage, as frequently it was found that she had stated what her husband gave her, which in some cases was strikingly different from that which he actually received.

Where the amount stated by the wife was what she actually received, and where it was found impossible to obtain any further information as to the husband's earnings, the wife's statement was used as a basis for forming an estimate of her husband's wage.

It was also found that sometimes in the cases of adult children, the mother would state what they gave her for board and lodging—usually about 10/- a week. Children when they first start usually hand over all their money to their parents, but in some cases they retain a few coppers for themselves.

In some cases the statement was very vague owing to the work being carried on at home or of such a character that it was almost impossible for any fixed wage to be stated. Such were the statements of the earnings of bargemen, rag and bone dealers, wood and salt hawkers and—in the case of women—charing and needlework. With the exception of such cases as these, the replies to the investigators' questions were of a definite charater. In those cases where information as to the wage was refused, it was found necessary to form an estimate. This did not prove a difficult task in a town of the size of Northampton, where in many of the trades and industries there are definite standard rates fixed by Trade Unions. Moreover, investigators were instructed to state the occupation with all practicable detail and to write on the back of the enquiry card any estimate or any additional information which would lead to an estimate. In the case of lads and girls, there was little likelihood of there being much difference between the estimated and actual earnings, while for adults it was practically certain to be within,

say, 5/–, and probably within a couple of shillings.[1]
It was only in a few instances, such as " son has a good
paper business in the evening, employing several boys,"
that we were baffled, and these cases were classified in
Tables relating to family income and earnings under
the heading " Unknown."

Where a large number of persons were found to be employed by a firm, the latter was asked to supply information as to the average weekly earnings (exclusive of overtime), of all the persons stated to be employed by them.
A quarter of the employers replied and their answers were
used to check the statements of the employees. A number
of persons could not be traced. This can easily be accounted for by the fact that the names forwarded to
employers were those of persons resident in the houses
at the time of the compilation of the directory ; in the
period intervening between this and the date of the
enquiry a number of removals are known to have taken
place. As no names were asked it was impossible to
know who made the statements without reference to the
directory.

Altogether the replies received from employers related
to 12 per cent. of the wage-earners. This percentage
is quite sufficient to show to what extent employees
overstated or understated their wages. First, as to
male workers, it was found that in nearly half the cases
the employee either stated his wage correctly or overstated it. Further, close upon three-quarters stated their
wages within two or three shillings ; but in a few instances
the difference between the employers' and employees'
statements was as much as ten shillings. With regard
to these latter cases it was found on further investigation
that some of them were men who at the time of the
enquiry were not earning the standard rate of the trade,

[1] The effect of this margin was carefully considered in compiling
the tables which follow.

but who were doing so when the employer replied; in other cases the employers' statements doubtless included overtime,[1] as is indicated by the fact that the statements of some firms were considerably above those of their employees in the case of nearly every individual; finally a very small proportion probably understated their wages considerably, but these are more than balanced by those who overstated their wage.

With women's wages agreement between the statements of employers and employees was closer still, for it was found that in three-fifths of the instances the wages were the same, whilst in four-fifths they were within one shilling. Only one woman understated her wages to any great extent.

Much the same may be said of the statements of girls and lads between the ages of 14 and 21 years. In more than three-quarters of the cases the statements may be relied upon to within a shilling. Serious differences arise only in the case of a few girls of the age of 16 and 17, and youths of 20, the probable cause being that when the enquiry was made fixed rates of wages were being earned, whereas at these ages they frequently commence to be paid piece-rates, and there is a consequent rise in the wage.

We can, then, conclude that on the whole there has been no general bias on the part of employees to understate or overstate the wages.

Only in individual cases is there likelihood of uncertainty, and where, in the opinion of the tabulators,[2] this uncertainty is serious, the household to which it applies has, in the Table relating to the poverty line, been classed above it in a group of " doubtfuls."

---

[1] In some cases employers definitely stated that they had included overtime, although they were requested not to do so.

[2] This opinion is formed upon a study of employers' statements and on a knowledge of the wages in operation in Northampton.

We now turn to the question of the usual rate of wages paid in various occupations.

Boot and Shoe Industry

In the shoe trade a boy of 14 years starts at 4/6, in some cases he gets 5/6 or a little more according to his intelligence. In a year's time he should be earning 7/– or 8/–. At the age of 17 he should receive about 13/–, although, as he increases in age, there is a tendency for the rate of wages to diverge, because employers reserve the right of freedom of contract with all work people under 18 years, and payment is made at piecework rates. Upon attaining the age of 18 years, however, he comes under the scale settled in the provisional agreement between the Federated Association of Boot and Shoe Manufacturers and the National Union of Boot and Shoe Operatives (January 26, 1909), which was in force at the time of the enquiry. This graduated scale is as follows :—

On attaining the age of 18 years   .. 18/– per week.
    ,,   ,,   19 years   .. 22/–   ,,
    ,,   ,,   20 years   .. 26/–   ,,
    ,,   ,,   21 years   .. 30/–   ,,

On attaining the age of 21, a workman may claim to receive the minimum of 30/–, but should an employer find that, in his opinion, a workman is not qualified to receive that rate, he then negotiates with the Trade Union officials and the two parties fix the wage. This accounts for the fact that in some cases shoe operatives over 21 years of age receive less than 30/– a week. It should be mentioned that the minimum rate of 30/– applies to the clicking, lasting, making and finishing, but not to the pressmen in the " rough stuff " department. Insole cutters usually get 28/–, and sometimes as little as 20/–.

Through the kindness of a leading manufacturer we have been able to tabulate the weekly earnings (during a certain week in the autumn) of all the male operatives in the clicking and making room. Under the term " making " is included welting and stitching, the processes which require the highest skilled workmen and which are accordingly the best paid.

TABLE V

AVERAGE WEEKLY WAGES PAID IN THE CLICKING AND MAKING DEPARTMENTS OF A BOOT AND SHOE FIRM

| ADULT MALES. | | LADS AND YOUTHS. | | | | | | | |
Weekly Wage.	No.	Weekly Wage.	13	14	15	16	17	18	19
Under 10/–	1, 1	4/– to 5/–	1	1, 5	..	..	..	..	..
10/– to 15/–	1	5/– „ 6/–	..	1, 2	..	..	..	..	..
15/– „ 19/–	2	6/– „ 7/–	..	1, 2	..	..	..	..	..
19/– „ 20/–	2	7/– „ 8/–	..	1	3, 2	..	1	..	..
20/– „ 21/–	..	8/– „ 9/–	..	1	3, 1	..	..	..	..
21/– „ 22/–	1, 1	9/– „ 10/–	..	..	1	2	..	..	..
22/– „ 23/–	2	10/– „ 11/–	..	..	1	..	1	..	..
23/– „ 24/–	2	11/– „ 12/–	..	..	..	3, 3	..	..	..
24/– „ 25/–	3, 2	12 — „ 13/–	..	..	1	1	1, 2	1	..
25/– „ 26/–	3, 2	13/– „ 14/–	..	..	..	2, 1	2	..	..
26/– „ 27/–	10, 2	14/– „ 15/–	..	..	..	..	2	..	..
27/– „ 28/–	..	15/– „ 16/–	1	..	..	..	1	1	..
28/– „ 29/–	3	16/– „ 17/–	..	..	..	1	1	..	..
29/– „ 30/–	1, 2	17/– „ 18/–	..	..	..	..	..	1, 1	..
30/– „ 31/–	7, 12	18/– „ 19/–	..	..	..	..	1	1	..
31/– „ 35/–	28, 13	19/– „ 20/–	..	..	..	..	..	3, 2	..
35/– „ 40/–	36, 12	20/– „ 21/–	..	..	..	..	..	..	1
40/– & over	14, 20	21/– „ 22/–	..	..	..	..	..	2	1, 2
		22/– „ 23/–	..	..	..	..	..	..	2
Total	113, 70	23/– „ 24/–	..	..	..	..	..	..	1
		24/– „ 25/–	..	..	..	..	..	..	..
		25/– „ 26/–	..	..	..	..	..	..	1

Figures in ordinary type refer to persons in the Clicking Department. Figures in black type refer to persons in the Making Department.

Next in size to the boot and shoe industry comes the building trade, the former employing five times as

many males as the latter.   The standard rates of wages
are as follows :—

Building Trade—   Wages and Summer Hours.

Bricklayers ..   ..⎫
Masons   ..   ..⎪ 9d. an hour for 53 hours, with
Carpenters & Joiners⎬ the exception of plasterers, who
Plumbers ..   ..⎪ work for 53 to 55 hours.
Plasterers ..   ..⎭

Slaters, 8½d. for 53 to 55 hours.

Painters, 8d. an hour for a week of 53 hours.

Labourers (Bricklayers, Masons and Plasterers), 6d. an
   hour for a week of 53 hours

Engineers—

Turners   ..⎫
Fitters   ..⎪
Planers   ..⎪ 34/- for week of 53 and 54 hours.
Smiths   ..⎬
Millwrights   ..⎪
Pattern-makers⎭
Planers   .. 32/- for week of 53 and 54 hours.

Ironfounders, 31/- for week of generally 53 and 54
   hours.

Printing[1]

WEEKLY RATES OF WAGES AND HOURS OF LABOUR

	CASE RATES.	MACHINE COMPOSING RATES.
Jobbing ..	33/6 (51 hours)	39/2* (51 hours)
Newspapers—		
Weekly ..	33/6	—
Evening ..	34/6 (51 hours)	37/6† (48 hours)

* Monotype.   † Linotype.

[1] According to a well-known Northampton printer the linotype
and monotype workers get 12 per cent. more than ordinary com-
positors, who average in Northampton about 34/6.   The latter

Furnishing—
   Cabinet Makers, 8½d. for 55 hours.
   French Polishers, 7d. for 55 hours.

Gas Workers—
   Gas Stokers (Hand), 4/6 per shift of 8 hours.
   „   „   (Machine), 5/4 per shift of 8 hours.

Police Constables, minimum, 25/- ; maximum, 36/6.
   In computing the average weekly earnings, some
allowance has been made for seasonal variations in hours
and for the loss of time caused by bad weather. For the
outdoor building occupations it has been assumed that
full time is nine-tenths of summer hours.

WOMEN'S WAGES

Boot and Shoe Industry.—A girl of 14 starting work
in a shoe factory is usually given work of a simple nature,
such as " knot tying." She would commence with a
wage of 4/6 or 5/-, and probably have a rise, usually 1/-,
at the end of six months. At the age of 16 she should
be getting 8/- or more, and when she was 18, if she were
working in the closing department, she would receive
wages on a graduated scale.

13/- at 18 years[1]	In some factories they receive
15/- at 19 years[1]	1/- less if on unimportant opera-
17/- at 20 years[1]	tions.

Girls in the shoe room, on the other hand, would receive

used to get the " night shilling," *i.e.*, an additional shilling for
work done after 10 p.m., but as they demanded this even if it
was for ¼ hour after 10 p.m., and a further shilling after mid-
night, it was opposed, and now the ordinary standard for overtime
is adopted. The " night shilling " originated from a shilling
granted for cheese and beer when shops were shut after 10 p.m.
It gradually developed into a recognised custom.

[1] We understand that since August, 1913, there has been a
rise of 1/- in each case.

from 12/- to 14/-, if over 18 years of age. Adult women would be receiving about 16/- or 17/-.

Blouse-making, etc.—A large number of young girls are employed in blouse-making, pinafore-making, and allied trades as learners. They start on a wage of 4/- or 4/6, and rise by increments of 6d. and 1/-. It is extremely difficult to state the wages that are usually obtained by girls of various ages, as some are placed on piece-work at quite an early age. We were informed, by one firm, that if a girl, on reaching the age of 18, was not in receipt of 13/- or 14/-, the girl was not as a rule kept. These wages, however, were found from our returns to be the amounts most usually received by girls of 18 and over, and by adult women. Taking the firms as a whole, the wages of girls of 18 were found to vary from 9/- to 14/-, and of adult women from 12/- to 18/-. The average wage of adult women was about 14/-.

Dressmaking.—A girl engaged in dressmaking frequently starts as an apprentice at a wage of 2/6 a week. Considerable variations exist in the wage of elder girls, but an adult worker may be expected to receive at least 10/- to 12/-, in many cases 15/- and more is obtained, a forewoman in one firm receiving £1 a week.

MEN'S EARNINGS

If one next studies earnings as a whole, quite irrespective of occupations, one obtains the results as found in Table VI. In this table is shown the distribution in the earnings of adult males.

The earnings tabulated have been those as stated by employees. It will be seen that, of married householders, there were 522 cases stated definitely, while the remaining 23 had to be estimated. The most general conclusions to be drawn from the table may be stated as follows :—

(1) That just under 10 per cent. of the married house-

TABLE VI—FULL-TIME WAGES OF ADULT MALES—ALL TRADES

NORMAL WEEKLY WAGE RATE.	MARRIED HOUSEHOLDERS.			Other Men over 20 Years, where known (including Lodgers).	TOTALS.
Number.	STATED.	ESTIMATED.	TOGETHER.		
	522	23	545	217	762
Under 18/-	26	3	29	22	51
18/- to 19/-	22	0	22	17	39
19/- ,, 20/-	3	0	3	1	4
20/- ,, 21/-	17	2	19	24	43
21/- ,, 22/-	9	0	9	3	12
22/- ,, 23/-	16	0	16	12	28
23/- ,, 24/-	14	1	15	11	26
24/- ,, 25/-	18	1	19	7	26
25/- ,, 26/-	27	1	28	17	45
26/- ,, 27/-	14	0	14	10	24
27/- ,, 28/-	18	3	21	8	29
28/- ,, 29/-	38	0	38	19	57
29/- ,, 30/-	5	0	5	0	5
30/- ,, 31/-	117	7	124	40	164
31/- ,, 35/-	60	0	60	11	71
35/- ,, 40/-	54	1	55	8	63
40/- and over	64	4	68	7	75

holders in Northampton among the wage-earning classes earn less than £1 a week, and about one-third between £1 and 30/– per week. On the other hand, just over 10 per cent. earn £2 a week or more.

(2) Nearly one in five of the males over 20 other than householders receive less than 20/– a week, while about one-half receive less than 25/– a week, and only 3½ per cent. over £2.

(3) In the final column of the table are given the earnings of all persons over 20 years of age, whether householders or not. Twelve per cent. earn less than £1 a week, just over one-half earn less than 30/– a week, and about 10 per cent. over £2 a week.

As the above table was based upon employees' statements, it would have been interesting to have compared it with the distribution of earnings as stated by employers. Unfortunately, the firms who sent information were, for the most part, such as employed one class of workers, namely, boot and shoe operatives ; hence the unskilled labourer appears to be in a considerably smaller proportion than should be the case if accurate information was procurable for all workers. Furthermore, the returns were made principally by the bigger employers of labour. Finally, such persons as worked on their own account, and as a result in many cases obtained irregular and frequently very low incomes, are not included

Family Income

Before coming to the question of the minimum standard, it is essential to tabulate the incomes of the families which form the subject of our study. As a great many difficulties arise as to what is and what is not income, it will be necessary to explain in some detail what is meant and what is included in the sequel under the term " family income."

First of all, the full-time wages of all earners in a

family are included,[1] on the assumption that they work
a full normal week,[2] together with any other earnings.
All persons temporarily unemployed (through illness
or any other cause), or under-employed, are regarded as
being in full employment for the reasons stated on p. 32.
Day servants and charwomen in private houses were
credited with their wages and sixpennyworth of food
per day ; while in cases of occasional charing or needlework, if there was no evidence to the contrary, it was
assumed that two days' work per week was done.
The rate of payment for charing was counted as 2/–
per day.

Further, to the sum of the income of individual members
of the household are added any pensions (State pensions
or others), any regular assistance from relatives, lodgers'
payments, and the rent from the ownership of property.
Lodgers' payment was thus treated. Where a lodger
was boarded and lodged, it was assumed that he con-
tributed one-third of the rent of the house ; in addition,
2/– of his weekly payments were regarded as wife's
earnings, and were, accordingly, added to the family
income. The remainder of his payment was assumed
to be spent on his board. Where the lodger merely had
rooms and no attendance, then he was regarded as paying
6d. to the household, and the remainder of his payment
as his share of the rent. Then the rent of the house,
less the lodger's contribution towards it, was regarded

[1] A family for this purpose was regarded as being composed of
all members who are related to the chief wage-earner or the head
of the family, and who were more or less permanent residents at
the house at the time of the enquiry. That is to say, it was
composed of all persons in the household except lodgers and
friends and relations paying temporary visits.

[2] Persons engaged in the outdoor building trade are assumed
to work 9/10 of the summer hours all the year round in order to
allow for the effects of bad weather and difference in hours. This
is probably an under-estimate of the time lost through these
causes.

as being the actual rent paid by the householder, and this latter was entered in Table VII. This accounts for the different distributions in rent, as shown in comparing Tables I. and VII.

A word of explanation is required on the subject of households owning property. Two distinct cases arise which need different methods of treatment. (*a*) When the owner lives in his own house, the amount he would have to pay if he rented it is added to his income—this gives his gross income. If his net income is required, one would have to subtract this amount plus the rates from his gross income. (*b*) When the owner does not live in his own house, the rents he receives for the houses less the amount paid by him in rates is added to his family income.

The relation between income and rent is shown in Table VII. on the next page.

The percentage of families with various amounts of income are as follows:—

Under 10/–	3 per cent.	} 8·5 per cent. of all working-class households,
10/– to 20/–	5·5 ,,	
20/– to 30/–		17 ,,
30/– to 35/–	19 ,,	} 30 ,,
35/– to 40/–	11 ,,	
40/– to 50/–		17 ,,
50/– to 60/–		9 ,,
60/– and over		16·5 ,,
Doubtful.		2 ,,

From this we see that the family income of about one-quarter of the working-class households in the town is less than 30/–, and that the family income of over half is less than £2 a week. The average is about 36/–. It is likely that incomes below 15/–, especially where the family is of any size, are supplemented by poor relief and charity; such irregular sources of income are diffi-

TABLE VII—Family Income and Rent

Weekly Rent (including rates and allowing for lodgers).	Under 10/-	10/- and under 15/-	15/- and under 20/-	20/- and under 25/-	25/- and under 30/-	30/- and under 35/-	35/- and under 40/-	40/- and under 45/-	45/- and under 50/-	50/- and under 55/-	55/- and under 60/-	60/- and over	Unknown	Total
Nil to 1/-	2	1	..	..	..	..	..	..	..	..	..	..	..	3
1/- to 1/9	4	..	..	..	..	..	..	..	..	..	..	..	..	4
2/- ,, 2/9	4	1	2	2	3	3	..	..	..	..	..	..	..	15
3/- ,, 3/9	2	2	8	11	7	11	7	5	1	1	2	3	..	60
4/- ,, 4/9	4	3	5	16	13	16	10	6	4	1	2	13	4	97
5/- ,, 5/9	2	5	6	5	21	30	18	19	11	6	12	28	4	167
6/- ,, 6/9	1	1	3	8	13	52	28	16	22	9	10	35	2	200
7/- ,, 7/9	..	1	..	2	13	17	10	10	7	8	2	24	3	97
8/- ,, 8/9	1	..	..	..	2	2	2	4	5	5	1	8	..	30
9/- ,, 9/9	..	..	..	..	..	..	2	1	4	2	..	2	..	11
10/- ,, 10/9	..	..	..	..	..	1	..	2	1	1	..	2	1	8
11/- ,, 11/9	..	..	..	..	..	..	..	..	1	..	..	..	..	1
12/-	..	..	..	..	..	..	..	..	..	..	..	..	..	..
Unknown ..	..	..	..	..	..	..	..	..	..	..	..	..	..	..
Total	20	14	24	44	72	132	77	63	56	33	29	115	14	693
Median income	5/3	12/-	17/3	23/-	27/6	30/3	36/-	41/-	47/-	51/-	56/-	76/-		
„ rent	2/11	4/9	4/-	4/6	5/6	6/-	6/-	6/-	6/6	6/9	5/8	6/11¼		
Rent as % of income	44	40	23	20	20	20	17	15	14	18	10	8		

cult to trace, and there are doubtless a few cases where they have not been disclosed.

The question of the relationship between income and rent is an important one. For incomes up to 35/- the relationship is close, but families with incomes above this amount show a great difference in the amount of rent they pay. As will be seen from the Tables there are three cases where the families have an income of over 60/-, whereas they only pay 3/- to 3/9 in rent. Further the high proportion which rent forms in the case of families with small incomes is strikingly shown, families with less than 15/- per week spending two-fifths of it in rent. Upon making a study of those families with insufficient incomes, it is found that food is allowed to fall below the necessary amount while a fairly good house (sometimes with more than the minimum accommodation) in a respectable street is rented.

Family Income and the Minimum Standard

Having definitely settled the family income in each case, we may now proceed to inquire the number of families where it is insufficient for the maintenance of physical health when in ordinary activity. For this purpose a standard of the minimum income which is requisite for the health of families of various sizes has to be established. This has already been done for more than one town. In the first instance it was carried out by Mr. Rowntree in his well-known book on York, in which he established a " poverty line " for that town in 1899. In these studies Mr. Rowntree's table is utilised, but modified to meet the prices current in each town at the date of the enquiry, and to allow for different needs for fuel and for compulsory insurance.

Mr. Rowntree's standard is based upon the cheapest rations authorised for use in workhouses and is mainly vegetarian and assumes that all children have equal needs.

It seemed advisable to devise an alternative standard of a more elastic nature and with a closer relation to actual methods of expenditure. The difference between the two standards is best explained as follows[1]:—" His (Mr. Rowntree's) minimum assumes perfectly scientific expenditure for obtaining necessary food constituents at the minimum cost. In fact, a workman would sacrifice part of the defined necessaries in favour of a meat diet. If we suppose about two pounds of meat bought per week, the additional expense of obtaining the same nourishment may, perhaps, be put at 9d. and the minimum food expenditure for preserving an adult workman in health and efficiency would then be 4/6. A new standard has been computed on this basis. In the York computation all children under 16 years were averaged together, and it seems better to take a more elastic diet as follows :—

Food Expenditure Basis.—100 = 4/6

	Males.	Females.		Males.	Females.
Over 18 years	100	80	5 to 14 years	50	50
16 to 18 years	85	80	0 to 5 years	33	33
14 to 16 years	85	70	Old-age pensioners ..	60	60

This gives 1/6 a week, one year with another, for a child under 5, and 2/3 a week on an average for children of school age. The relative scale is akin to that suggested by various authorities. Careful consideration of expenditure and prices in Reading supports the view that these sums spent judiciously, but on the commodities usually purchased, would just supply a minimum sufficiency of nourishment."

This new food scale makes a greater allowance for adults and less for young children. This food expenditure basis,

[1] From *Statistical Journal*, 1912-13, p. 684.

together with the same scale for clothing and sundries as used by Mr. Rowntree, forms the New Standard used in the subsequent Tables.

The modifications which it was necessary to make in order to apply the standards to Northampton were not great in relation to food and fuel. So far as comparison could be drawn it was found that prices in Northampton in 1913 were about 16 per cent. higher for food than in York when Mr. Rowntree carried out his enquiry. The price as well as consumption of coal in Northampton compared with that in York leads to a much lower standard of expenditure on fuel, which is to some extent balanced by the compulsory payment for State Insurance as is shown in the Tables given below.

We have now to determine the number of families living below and above the standards. Our first step is to subtract from the family income the rent[1] and the amount paid in State Insurance for each person falling under Parts I. and II. of the National Health Insurance Act. The remainder then forms the amount available for expenditure.

It is assumed, however, that the whole of this remainder is spent on commodities essential for the physical health of the family. No allowance is made for expenditure on such items as tram fares, insurance other than State, tobacco, beer, petty luxuries, amusements, betting, nor for pocket money of any kind. On the other hand, we have not included any benefit derived from allotments (there are large numbers of allotment holders in Northampton, who at the expense of a rent of 6d. to 9d. a pole, save a perceptible proportion of their food bill), nor the occasional petty earnings of members of the family.

---

[1] Following the example of Mr. Rowntree we have subtracted rent first on the assumption that in cases of poverty it is unlikely that a family will pay more than the necessary minimum on this form of expenditure, though cases occur.

F

TABLE VIII

STANDARDS FOR TYPICAL HOUSEHOLDS

	Fuel and State Insurance.	Clothing and Sundries.	Food. Rowntree Standard.	Food. New Standard.	Total (excluding rent). Rowntree Standard.	Total (excluding rent). New Standard.
	s. d.	s. d.	s. d.	s. d.	s. d.	s. d.
Man and wife	1 7	1 4	7 0	8 2	9 11	11 1
Man, wife and two school children ..	1 7	2 6	12 2	12 8	16 3	16 9
Man, wife and three children under 5 years	1 7	3 1	14 9	12 8	19 5	17 4
Add for each man 18 years	..	3 8	3 6	4 6	..	..
" " woman over 16 ..	..	0 8	3 6	4 6	..	..
" " girl; 14 to 16 ..	..	0 8	3 6	3 8	..	..
" " lad; 16 to 18 ..	..	0 7	2 7	3 8	..	..
" " boy; 14 to 16 ..	..	0 8	3 6	3 10	..	..
" " school child; 5 to 14	..	0 7	2 7	3 10	..	..
" " infant under 5 ..	..	0 7	2 7	2 3	..	..
				1 6		

In addition, as pointed out previously, the earnings of members of a family have been calculated on the assumption that they are fully employed, except in the case of persons engaged in the building trade. Although a man or a member of his family may at the time of the enquiry be unemployed, he is regarded as being in full employment, unless he is permanently unemployed or incapacitated. Hence the poverty test in this case is more lenient than that which Mr. Rowntree adopted in the case of York, as he studied annual earnings, in which case the overtime would probably in most cases be less than the time spent in broken time and holidays. If the remainder of the income, after rent and insurance have been deducted, is greater than the amount necessary for the physical health of the family as established in both standards of Table VIII., then the family is above the poverty line ; if less, then the family is below it. It is of course possible that a family may be above one standard and yet be below the other.

Using these methods we find that 57 families out of a total of 693 are below the Rowntree Poverty Standard. (In addition to these there are a number of others that are possibly below.) That is to say, about 8 per cent. of the working-class families in our sample are below the poverty line. Furthermore, these 57 families contain 9 per cent. of the working-class population which fell within the scope of the enquiry. Hence we may say that from 8 per cent. to 9 per cent. of the working-class population, so far as they are dependent on pensions, earnings and all income other than poor relief or charity, are below the level necessary for the maintenance of physical health. This percentage compares very favourably with the corresponding one for York (1899), which was 15½ per cent., and still more favourably with Reading (1912), which was 25 to 30 per cent.

The number of persons who are near the poverty line

cannot be gathered from the above figures, for a further analysis reveals that there were 4 probably below the standard, whilst there were 13 cases where it is difficult to determine whether the family was above or below, so they were classed as doubtful. On the other hand the statement must not be assumed to mean that 8 to 9 per cent. were destitute or in acute poverty ; for in a number of cases poor relief is given (out of these 57 families it is known to be given in 10 cases and it is quite possible that there are other recipients who have hidden the fact from the investigator), and in some cases absent children and other relatives assist. As a matter of fact this is definitely stated to be the case with one household ; a woman who receives parish relief states that her daughter will not see her suffer and therefore pays the extra amount that she requires.

In Table IV^x. (Appendix) p. 207 is a classification of households according to earners on the basis of the two standards. The earlier part of the main grouping of the table is given in summary below :—

Earners.	Number of Households.	Number of Households Below New Standard.
Man alone	267	21
,, and one son or daughter ..	89	7
,, and two sons or daughters ..	69	1
,, and three sons or daughters..	40	1
,, and four or more ,, ..	26	0

It is seen that in the group " man alone earning " and in the following group about 8 per cent. of the households are below the poverty line ; this percentage falls as the number of children who assist in maintaining the family increases, to 1 or 2 in the third and fourth groups and zero in the fifth. We also find that our results in another way indicate that as the number of children at work increases the percentage of families falling below the standard decreases—thus, in the case of the 573 households headed by an adult male wage-earner the percentage is 6, as compared with 15 in the case of those households where the sole wage-earner has two or more children dependent.

The same table shows that 11 of the 93 households, where through the death or incapacity of the husband the widow or wife and her children have to earn, are below the poverty line, that is to say, 12 per cent. are below.

Households below the Poverty Line.—If a study be made of the 57 households below the poverty line, it will be found that in a third of them there is only one adult man earning and he has, in every case except two, to support his wife and three or more children.

The households are composed of persons as analysed in Table IX.

It will be seen that nearly half the wage-earners below the line are women and children, and that a quarter of the adult men are non-wage-earners.

As to the occupations of the male wage-earners who owe their position below the minimum standard to low wages, it is found that over a third of them are unskilled labourers, a few are casual labourers, a few shopkeepers' assistants—there are also a couple who are shoe operatives working at home (a survival of the old system of boot manufacture which was killed by the advent of machinery). Many of these old hand-workers are suffering great hardships at the present time ; they cannot take to a new industry because in many cases they are too old ; they have merely to live on as best they can or go into the workhouse.

As to the immediate causes of the deficiency in those incomes which fall below the Rowntree standard, it is often very difficult to assign a precise cause, because in some

TABLE IX

	EARNING.						
	Men over 20.	Women over 16.	Girls 14–16.	Sons 18–20.	Lads and Boys 14–18.	School Children under 14.	Total.
Below New Standard ..	34	19	3	2	1	2	61
Total	805	364	40	72	121	5	1,407
Percentage below ..	4	5	7	3	1	—	4·4

	DEPENDENT.						
	Men over 18.	Women.	Girls.	Lads and Boys.	School Children.	Infants.	Total.
Below New Standard ..	13	50	2	1	91	48	205
Total	60	644	14	8	570	278	1,574
Percentage below ..	22	8	—	—	16	17	13

	EARNING AND DEPENDENT.				
	Men.	Women.	Girls, Lads, and Boys over 14.	Children and Infants under 14.	All.
Percentage below ..	5	7	4	16½	9

Persons below, 266 ; persons above, 2,715 ; total, 2,981.

Ward.	Number of Cases.	Proportion to Number of Habitable Working Class Houses in our Sample.
South	8	1 in 7
North	9	1 in 9
Kingsthorpe	7	1 in 9
Castle	10	1 in 10
St. Michael	5	1 in 12
St. Lawrence	4	1 in 13
St. Edmund	4	1 in 17½
St. Crispin	3	1 in 20
Far Cotton	2	1 in 22
Abington	2	1 in 25
St. James	2	1 in 36
Kingsley	1	1 in 44

cases two factors are operating to drag the family down. However, for the purposes of comparison the line has been drawn as definitely as possible, and in cases of doubt the cause which appears to be predominant has been assumed to be the only one. The percentages of households below the standard through different causes is given in Chapter I., p. 40.

Low wages, it will be seen, are not so great a cause of the deficiency in Northampton as in the two other towns, though they are still the predominant cause. In over a third of the total number of cases, the families are placed in straitened circumstances through the death, old age or incapacity of the chief breadwinner. In another 35 per cent. of the cases the cause is the largeness of the family; in some of these instances high wages are being earned, but these are more than counterbalanced by the fact that the family contains five, six or seven children of school age or under.

TABLE X

FAMILIES ABOVE AND BELOW THE POVERTY LINE

RELATION TO MR. ROWNTREE'S STANDARD.				RELATION TO NEW STANDARD.			
Above.	No. of Households.	Below.	No. of Households.	Above.	No. of Households.	Below.	No. of Households.
shillings		shillings		shillings		shillings	
+ 40 ..	111	−15 to 16	..	+ 40 ..	102	− 9 ,, 10	2
+ 35 to 40	27	−14 ,, 15	..	+ 35 to 40	30	− 8 ,, 9	2
+ 30 ,, 35	46	−13 ,, 14	..	+ 30 ,, 35	39	− 7 ,, 8	2
+ 25 ,, 30	76	−12 ,, 13	..	+ 25 ,, 30	64	− 6 ,, 7	2
+ 20 ,, 25	..	−11 ,, 12	1	+ 20 ,, 25	86	− 5 ,, 6	3
+ 18 ,, 20	92	−10 ,, 11	..	+ 18 ,, 20	47	− 4 ,, 5	6
+ 16 ,, 18	27	− 9 ,, 10	1	+ 16 ,, 18	46	− 3 ,, 4	9
+ 14 ,, 16	48	− 8 ,, 9	2	+ 14 ,, 16	44	− 2 ,, 3	4
+ 12 ,, 14	48	− 7 ,, 8	5	+ 12 ,, 14	41	− 1 ,, 2	9
+ 10 ,, 12	30	− 6 ,, 7	3	+ 10 ,, 12	31	− 0 ,, 1	8
+ 8 ,, 10	32	− 5 ,, 6	2	+ 8 ,, 10	35	Amnt. not known	6
+ 7 ,, 8	24	− 4 ,, 5	3	+ 7 ,, 8	11		
+ 6 ,, 7	13	− 3 ,, 4	11	+ 6 ,, 7	12	..	..
+ 5 ,, 6	10	− 2 ,, 3	8	+ 5 ,, 6	5	..	..
+ 4 ,, 5	6	− 1 ,, 2	8	+ 4 ,, 5	..	..	..
+ 3 ,, 4	3	− 0 ,, 1	7	+ 3 ,, 4	..		
+ 2 ,, 3	..	Amnt. not known.	6	+ 2 ,, 3	..	..	..
+ 1 ,, 2	2	..	..	+ 1 ,, 2	..		
+ 0 ,, 1	2	..	..	+ 0 ,, 1	6	..	..
Amnt. not known	15	..	..	Amnt. not known	17		
	7	..	..		7		
Total	619	..	—	..	623	..	53

Also probably below 4 and possibly 13.

Of peculiar interest is the classification of the households below the poverty line according to the wards of the borough in which they are situated. It will be remembered that reference was made in the section on Housing to the evil conditions in the older portion of the town: North, South and Castle Wards. Owing to the bad housing in these districts, rents are low, and they thus attract the poorer families. As a consequence one would expect to find that a large proportion of these families were below the standard, and that this is so is shown on p. 87.

In Table X. the distribution of households according to the amount of income by which they differ from the two standards is given.

Budgets

A few families were asked to keep budgets, not in order to investigate distribution of expenditure in general, but mainly for the purpose of obtaining statements of the price of articles most commonly consumed by the wage-earning classes. The classification of households has shown already that in our sample there are 330 kinds of households. Hence it is extremely difficult to get information from " typical families," for these can hardly be said to exist. Further, even if such a family were to be found, there are many and great differences in the directions in which the family income can be spent. Then again, in most cases the family which is living well is the only one to be found to keep a budget satisfactorily. Just those families about whom one desires to obtain details of family expenditure either cannot or will not collect and give the information. Hence a large number of budgets has not been collected, and the few that have were utilised for the above-mentioned purpose. It is of interest, however, to insert the broad lines of expenditure in each of these cases, as well as a description of the families giving the information :—

Family A is composed of a widow (age about 30) with four daughters (6, 3, and 2 years, and an infant of 10 months). The woman is unable to go out to work owing to the size and age of her family. Her sole means of support is 13/6 parish relief. This, as will be seen, is below the amount necessary to keep her and her family in physical health. According to the Rowntree standard

she should receive 18/1, besides rent, and according to
the New standard 14/8. The house in which she lives is
a three-roomed one with no garden. The food expenditure, which is given in the table below, may be sub-
divided as follows :—

Butcher ..	..	..	8d.
Baker ..	..	..	3/9
Milkman	..	..	2/1
Fishmonger	..	..	4d.
Greengrocer	..	..	4d.
Grocer ..	..	..	1/5
			8/7

The large milk bill is explained by the youngsters being
ill and requiring milk.

Family B is composed of a man (age about 60), wife
of about the same age, two daughters (30 and 27 years),
and two sons (22 and 18 years). The man is a railway
signalman, and earns 23/–. The daughter of 30 does
dressmaking at home, and must earn about 10/– a week,
though she gives her mother 6/– or 7/–, according to her
earnings. The daughter of 27 is a stationery assistant,
who pays 5/– for her board—she refused to reveal her
wages, as also did the sons, but she would probably get
about 12/–. The two sons are both clerks, and pay their
mother 10/– a week each for their board—the wages of
the elder son would probably be about 30/–, and of the
younger one about £1. The family rent an allotment,
for which they pay 10/– a year. Their house is one of
six rooms with a rent of 6/– a week. The family is typical
of a well-to-do working-class household, where through the
children earning, the family is comfortably off. The
family is also " rising," that is, the children are entering
upon clerical work, and have not followed their family in
skilled manual work.

Family C is composed of a man (34), wife, two daughters (7 and 3), and four sons (13, 11, 5 and 1). The man is a warehouseman, and is in receipt of a weekly wage of £1 a week, out of which he gives his wife 19/–. In addition to this amount, a lodger pays the family 1/– per week for renting a room.

	A.		B.		C.	
	Actual Expenditure.	New Standard.	Actual Expenditure.	New Standard.	Actual Expenditure.	New Standard.
	s. d.	s. d.	s. d.	s. d.	s. d.	s. d.
Rent	4 3	3 0	6 0	6 0	5 0	5 0
Clothes	0 5½	2 2	3 0	3 0	..	3 6
Fuel and State Insurance	1 3	1 3	4 0	2 6	2 3	1 7
Food	8 7	10 5	33 6	24 6	13 4	20 2
Other expenditure	0 6½	0 10	8 0	1 0	0 11	1 4
Total	15 1	17 8	54 6	37 0	21 6	31 7
Income[1]	13 6	..	54 6	..	22 0	..

[1] Including the whole of the lodger's payments.

Rent is here computed for the New Standard as that of the cheapest house which would give one room per "equivalent adult" (p. 56 and 60).

CHAPTER III

WARRINGTON, the second in our series of surveys, is a striking contrast to Northampton. Unlike that city, it possesses a diversity of industry which is seldom to be found in so limited an area. The reason of this diversity is not far to seek, for very few towns have the advantages Warrington possesses. Situated on the Mersey, and on the fringe of the South Lancashire coalfield, it is able, in a short space of time, to obtain its raw material from, and to despatch the finished product to, two of the biggest commercial and industrial centres (Liverpool and Manchester) in the country. These two cities are within twenty miles of Warrington. Railway communication is very good, three lines passing through the town, while with the Manchester Ship Canal at hand and level roads in the neighbourhood, a considerable proportion of traffic is by water and road. Warrington receives special advantages from the Manchester Ship Canal Company on account of the support it gave to the scheme of construction when it was first brought forward.

These advantages attract a very large number of industries to the town. There are in Warrington some of the largest ironworks in the United Kingdom. There are also several wireworks, where the processes of wire drawing and weaving are carried out. Firms manufacturing bedsteads, tubes, boilers and engines, and two of the largest gas-stove works in the country are established there. A well-known firm of soap manufacturers employs a large number of persons. In addition there are tanneries, a cotton mill, fustian-cutting factories and breweries. Other important trades are those in boxes, printing, glass, rubber, flour, white lead, timber and building materials. With so many industries upon which it may be dependent, the town escapes comparatively lightly when one or a few of its trades are suffering from commercial depression or the results of a strike.

But the town possesses striking disadvantages when we compare it with other industrial areas. Northampton, for a manufacturing town, is remarkably clean ; the boot and shoe factories do not require tall chimneys pouring out dense volumes of smoke, and the number of factories from which pollution takes place is very small. Warrington, on the other hand, is at times " one mass of smoke." That this evil is realised by the inhabitants themselves is shown by the articles and letters which have appeared on this subject in the local press as a result of a report issued by the Smoke Abatement League. It is remarked by one correspondent that if any one wishes to know what Warrington might look like, let him note its appearance on Sundays when the works are at rest, and the sun is not obscured by the smoke of so many chimneys. No one pretends that this smoke could be abolished entirely, but in a leading article of one of the local papers, it is stated on the authority of " a practical man—a master who knows as much about iron-works conditions as most men—that nine-tenths of the smoke that now blackens the skies and pollutes the air by which we live could be avoided." The local authorities were at the time of our enquiry contemplating action in the matter. It is probable that it has already been taken.

In drawing a further comparison of Warrington with Northampton it might be noted that the diversity of industry in the former results in a diversity of living, which is not found to the same extent in the midland town and which has to be taken into account when the welfare of households is considered. For instance, the expenditure which the ironworker has to incur in order to keep his wife and family in health is greater than the necessary expenditure of a textile operative. The causes of this difference are indicated in the section on earnings.

Numerous contrasts could be drawn between the two towns, but for our purpose the above serve to show that the areas are entirely dissimilar.

The study of Warrington was carried out in the early autumn of 1913, the bulk of it being made during the first fortnight of September. Conditions of employment at the time may, on the whole, be regarded as being normal, although towards the end of the period short time was being worked in some of the ironworks. Persons specially qualified to give an opinion have been approached as to a description of the state of employment in September and the replies have been quoted in detail below :—

" With one or two exceptions, the condition of trade in Warrington in September, 1913, would be accurately described as ' normal,' that is to say, the bulk of the industries in the town were jogging steadily along, and would not call for outstanding comment. The exceptions would be :—

"   (1) The Fustian and Velvet Cutting Industry.
"   (2) The Soap Industry.
"   (3) The Gas Stove and Range Industry.

And the following is an outline of the position in these industries :—

" *Fustian and Velvet Cutting.*—In September of last year a depression had begun in this industry which still obtains (March, 1914), with the result that a large number of cutters were displaced, mainly females.

This is due to the fact that velvets, which had been for some time very fashionable, have now made way for some other material, and in addition machines are being introduced to do the work which was formerly done by hand.

" *Soap.*—The condition of this industry in September could best be described as quiet. On the other hand, this is a condition which always obtains at that time of the year, and, therefore, the state of the trade could not be described as anything out of the ordinary.

" *Gas Stove and Range Industry.*—The industry at the time of the enquiry was very busy, and just reaching a position when a downward tendency could be expected. For the first nine months of 1913 the industry had been very much busier than it had been during the previous year, and as a result a larger number of men were employed at the work than had been the case previously, and extensions of the works at both firms had been made to cope with the additional orders."

Taking everything into consideration, then, we should not be wrong in assuming trade to have been normal during the period of our enquiry. Moreover, as we pointed out in the previous chapter, short time and overtime do not affect our results, for they are disregarded, and all persons are assumed to be in full employment, except builders.[1] The reader must allow for this fact in calculating annual earnings.

The selection of houses was made in much the same way in both towns, except that instead of the directory we used the list of houses assessed at various rates.

[1] Throughout the whole of this chapter the methods of and rules for classification that have been used are the same as those described in the previous one. Hence it will be unnecessary to describe them in detail afresh. Attention will only be drawn to those cases where new methods have been introduced.

These houses were arranged in alphabetical order, and the mode of selecting the "one in twenty" was the same as that adopted in Northampton. Of the 826 dwellings marked off, 139 were found to be shops and 13 the houses of principal residents. The investigators called upon the remaining 674, and in the end obtained information from all but 2 of them, in both of which the occupants could be stated to belong to a "superior class." Further, on examination of the 674, it was found that 7 more were shops and 27 (including the two unknowns) were "superior," that is to say, the occupiers were clerks, professional men, travellers, shop managers, etc. Hence 640 households of the wage-earning class were investigated.

The number of houses of a superior class in Warrington is relatively much smaller than in Reading or Northampton, for many persons occupied in Warrington live in a pleasanter district south of the borough.

Information as to the number of inhabited houses, etc., is to be found in the Census Reports, but relates to April, 1911 :—

	Number.	Population.
Inhabited dwelling-houses and flats..	13,002	65,011
Empty	678	—
Inhabited shops	881	4,199
Hotels, etc., offices, workshops, etc., and miscellaneous	135	743
Institutions	28	2,147
Uninhabited buildings	89	—
	14,813	72,100[1]

[1] In addition there were 66 persons on vessels, sheds, etc., or vagrants.

As building operations in Warrington have been slack in recent years, it is probable that the number of inhabited dwelling-houses was about the same as in April, 1911, at any rate not more than 13,200. Since then 680 residences fell within the scope of the enquiry, our sample was of 1 house in 19.3. This multiplier 19⅓ will have to be applied to all sample data if an estimate for the whole borough is required.

Housing

Housing conditions are very varied in Warrington, as one would expect in a town of such antiquity. The general appearance of workmen's dwellings gives one the impression that they are considerably older here than those in Northampton, where street after street of red brick and apparently newly-constructed residences are to be found. Compared with Northampton, Warrington looks somewhat desolate. " In the older and central portion (of the town), comprising chiefly Town Hall, Howley and St. John's Wards, are narrow streets and back courts and alleys containing insanitary dwellings, now gradually disappearing, partly through street widening, partly through the work of the Health Committee. Shops and offices are largely supplanting residences in the middle of the town. Around this is an area of streets of small houses called into existence by the industrial development of the last fifty years. . . . Much of the property of twenty years ago or more has passed into a very bad state through the absence of damp course, etc."[1] A stranger is struck with the appalling condition of some of the houses comprising the courts off Winwick Road, also the dwellings in the neighbourhood of Brick Street, Ship Yard, etc. Within easy distance of these streets houses are to be found which are described by investigators as follows :—

[1] Annual Report of the Medical Officer of Health for Warrington, 1912, p. 22.

G

(1) Very poor house, low neighbourhood, dirty, no outlook, very much enclosed; in fact, daylight is most scanty.

(2) The street, or, rather, narrow (10 ft.) passage, only contains four houses and ends in a *cul de sac*. All the walls of the houses are colour-washed, the floors are flagged and the ceilings very low owing to the age of the property. It is situated in an extremely poor district.

(3) The house was in fairly good condition, but rather small—practically no yard. Street probably narrowest in town, 10 ft. from wall to wall, 6 ft. from footpath to footpath.

(4) This house is in a terribly low neighbourhood. It is approached by a 3½-ft. alley and forms one of a row of 4 in a small back square. Property very old, shocking condition, hardly any windows intact, tiled floor with large holes in it. The rent has just been raised from 2/- to 2/6. This house is the largest (4 rooms) in the row; the others having only one room up and one down. The conveniences are built at the side and are used by the whole of the tenants of the square.

Numerous other cases could be quoted but the above are sufficient to give one an idea of some of the existing property and a picture of some of the congested areas which exist in the town. That this state of affairs could be remedied is beyond question, for close at hand to these districts and in the very heart of the town, are large areas of entirely unoccupied land.

Moreover these congested areas develop slums. That there are large numbers of slum dwellings[1] is revealed by enquiries instituted by the local authorities in 1911. Vital statistics for the twelve months were calculated for the population living in these dwellings, and the results,

[1] " Dwellings which open into courts or which are so situated in back or badly ventilated streets as to be under . . . . insanitary conditions."

which were published in the Report of the Medical Officer
of Health, are quoted below, together with the similar
statistics for the year 1907. " The population dealt with
in calculating the slum rates is a small one, and therefore,
some reserve must be exercised when referring to the
figures. The figures, however, certainly show that there
is a high mortality among those dwellings in this class of
property."

	1907.		1911.	
	Whole Borough.	Slums.	Whole Borough.	Slums.
Number of houses (total) ..	14,049	425	14,890	339
„ „ (without through ventilation) ..	..	236	..	74
Number of houses with only one entrance but through ventilation	..	56	..	107
Population	71,849	1,316[1]	72,375	1,175[2]
Birth-rate per 1,000 population	32·7	54·7	28·1	35·6
Death-rate per 1,000 population	15·7	53·1	16·9	26·3
Zymotic death-rate per 1,000 population	2·1	7·6	2·8	8·5
Infantile death-rate per 1,000 births	122	263	147	285
Diarrhœa death-rate of children under 1 year per 1,000 births	16·9	27·7	40·7	47·6

[1] 64 under 1 year.   [2] 41 under 1 year.

The above figures speak for themselves. But it is
necessary to emphasize specially a few of the facts
revealed by the above Table. In the first place, despite
the fact that the death-rate for the borough as a whole
was higher in 1911 than it was in 1907, yet the mortality
in the slum area is only half the amount it was at the
earlier date. Again, the increase of infantile mortality in

slum areas is relatively no greater than that in the
borough as a whole in 1911 than in 1907. Finally, during
the space of four years (1907-11), the number of slum
houses has been reduced by a fifth. Further activities
upon the part of the Council since that period are shown
by the following statistics compiled from the data supplied in the Medical Officer's Reports :—

	Closed.	Demolished.	Improved.
1911	71[1]	20	119
1912	21	—	32

Although much has been done by the local authorities
still more remains to be done. Where demolitions have
taken place, model workmen's dwellings might be
erected instead of allowing the land to remain a hideous
waste and an eye-sore to every one. Further, a policy of
systematic town planning could quite possibly be carried
out if the ratepayers would stir in this matter. It is
obviously one which is of vital importance to the welfare
of the town.

We may now turn to the tabulation of the statements
made in the house-to-house visitations. The first table
for consideration is that showing the relationship between
the rent (including rates) of houses and the number of
rooms they contain.

It will be noticed that 44 per cent. of the houses have a
rental of 4/- to 4/9 ; 20 per cent. have a rental of 5/- to 5/9 ;
and the rent is 3/- to 3/9 in about 15 per cent. of the cases.
Comparing this with Northampton we find that whereas in
the Midland town 70 per cent. of the households pay 5/-
to 7/9 in rent, only half that percentage pay as much in
Warrington. Another point worthy of notice is that more
than half the houses contain four rooms. The four-
roomed house is, in fact, the predominant type in Warrington, and these are mostly rented at from 4/- to 4/9

---

[1] Of these 24 were demolished and 2 improved in 1912.

TABLE I

NUMBER OF WORKING-CLASS HOUSES CLASSIFIED ACCORD-
ING TO RENTS AND ROOMS

Weekly Rents (including Rates.)	NUMBER OF ROOMS.										Totals.
	1	2	3	4	5	6	7	8	9	10	
2/- to 2/9	..	3	2	6	..	..	..	..	..	..	11
3/- ,, 3/9	..	4	12	73	2	2	..	..	..	..	93
4/- ,, 4/9	..	1	13	211	39	18	..	..	..	..	282
5/- ,, 5/9	..	..	..	28	57	51	..	..	..	..	136
6/- ,, 6/9	..	..	..	2	18	39	3	..	..	..	62
7/- ,, 7/9	..	..	..	..	3	25	1	1	..	..	30
8/- ,, 8/9	..	..	..	..	..	6	3	1	..	1	11
9/- ,, 9/9	..	..	..	..	..	3	1	1	..	..	5
10/- ,, 10/9	..	..	..	..	1	4	..	..	..	..	5
11/- ,, 11/9	..	..	..	..	..	..	..	1	..	..	1
12/-	..	..	..	..	..	..	..	1	..	..	1
Totals	..	8	27	320	120	148	8	5	..	1	637
Median Rent	..	3/-	3/9	4/3	5/-	6/-	7/9	9/-	..	..	4/6

though quite a fair number are rented at 3/– to 3/9, and
a few at 5/– to 5/9. For the five-roomed house the tenant
pays in nearly half the cases 5/– to 5/9, whilst six-roomed
houses for the most part vary from 5/– to 6/9. That the
Board of Trade figures support these conclusions is seen
from the comparison drawn below :—

	3-Roomed House.	4-Roomed House.	5-Roomed House.	6-Roomed House.
Board of Trade..	3/– to 4/6	4/– to 5/–	5/– to 5/6	—
Warrington Enquiry	3/– to 4/9	4/– to 4/9	5/– to 5/9	5/– to 6/9

It must be remembered, however, that the Board of
Trade figures refer to May, 1912, and those of the
Enquiry to September, 1913.

The types of houses are described by the Board of
Trade in the following words, " Two-storied houses of

three, four and five rooms are those usually occupied. A five-roomed house has a parlour and living-room on the ground floor and three bedrooms, one over the scullery, upstairs. Some of the four-roomed houses have a built-out scullery, with a bedroom over it; in others there is no separate scullery, the places of the parlour and the living-room being taken by the living-room and 'back kitchen.' Houses of the latter type in which the so-called 'back kitchen' is merely of scullery accommodation have been classed as three-roomed. Most houses are flat fronted and lack forecourt; In the smaller ones there is usually a lobby instead of a front passage. Each house has a separate yard, from which access is obtained by a back lane."

As not only the number of rooms but the height and size of houses are matters of importance, certain typical houses at four of the commonest rents were selected, and measurements of their rooms were made. These measurements are summarised in Appendix Table I.^{w}, p. 188.

TABLE II

NUMBER OF WORKING-CLASS HOUSES CLASSIFIED ACCORDING TO THE NUMBERS OF PERSONS AND OF ROOMS

No. of Rooms	NUMBER OF PERSONS IN HOUSE.												Totals.
	1	2	3	4	5	6	7	8	9	10	11	12	
I	..	..	..	..	..	..	..	..	..	..	..	..	..
2	2	3	..	1	1	1	..	..	..	..	..	..	8
3	..	3	7	2	7	4	2	2	..	..	..	..	27
4	2	43	49	77	62	41	26	11	10	..	..	..	321
5	1	11	16	21	23	19	12	6	5	3	4	..	121
6	..	14	26	31	25	14	11	10	8	4	4	1	148
7	..	1	..	3	2	1	..	..	1	..	..	..	8
8	..	..	..	..	2	1	..	..	2	..	..	..	5
9	..	..	..	..	..	..	..	..	..	..	..	..	..
10	..	..	..	..	..	..	1	..	..	..	..	..	1
Totals:	5	75	98	135	122	81	52	29	26	7	8	1	639

Table II. shows us the number of persons in relation to the number of rooms. Adopting the same definition of overcrowding as was used in the case of Northampton, viz., the census definition of more than two persons to a room, we find that there are 20[1] cases in which this takes place out of a total of 639. That is to say, according to this definition, there was overcrowding in 3 per cent. of the households of Warrington, whereas the Census returns show nearly double this amount of overcrowding. This difference is possibly due to the fact that in parts of Lancashire, including Warrington, the line of demarcation between a kitchen and scullery is very slight, and it is probable that in many instances the unofficial investigators regarded such a room as a kitchen (and hence for our purposes, a room), whereas the Census enumerators termed it a scullery. For the purposes of both enquiries a scullery was regarded as not being a room—in the sense that it is not a living-room and does not afford floor space for sleeping accommodation.

That the above reason is probably the cause of the difference in the percentage of overcrowding will be seen by comparing the results of the official and unofficial investigators as to the number of rooms in a dwelling.

A comparison with the Census Report on Tenements (Vol. VIII.) is permissible, as Warrington may be regarded as being almost entirely a working-class town, for the residences of the professional and upper classes of Warrington lie for the most part outside the borough.

It is found that the number of houses with varying sizes of rooms are as follows :—

[1] In 20 other cases there are exactly two persons to a room, while in the remaining 599 there are less than two occupants to a room.

| Rooms. | Houses. | Percentage. | |
		Official.	Unofficial.
1	60	·1	
2	1,325	1·9	
3	9,587	13·7	4·7
4	24,688	35·4	50·0
5	22,606	32·4 } 92·0	19·4 } 97·0
6	7,344	10·5	22·9
7	1,853	2·7	
8	1,048	1·5	
9	563	·8	
10 and more	708	1·0	
	69,782	100·0	

The difference may also be partly due to the fact that a number of smaller-roomed houses have been closed or demolished since 1911, while large-roomed houses have since been built. But this is not likely to affect the result except to a very slight extent, as building operations have not been active in Warrington in recent years.

The purpose of Table III. is to show the amount of overcrowding according to the more elastic standard explained on p. 22. It is seen that in 126 cases out of 639, that is in nearly 20 per cent. of the households, there is overcrowding according to the definition there described viz., more than one equivalent adult to a room. In 51 other cases the standard is reached, and in the remaining 462 cases more than sufficient room is to be found.

While the latter portion of our enquiry was in progress,

TABLE III

NUMBER OF WORKING-CLASS HOUSES CLASSIFIED ACCORDING TO THE NUMBER OF EQUIVALENT ADULTS AND OF ROOMS

No. of Rooms.	NUMBER OF EQUIVALENT ADULTS IN HOUSES.																
	1	1½	1¾	2	2¼	2½	2¾	3	3¼	3½	3¾	4	4¼	4½	4¾	5	5¼
1	..	..	..	..	..	..	..	..	..	..	..	..	..	..	..	..	..
2	2	..	1	2	1	..	1	..	..	..	..	1	..	..	..	..	..
3	..	..	..	3	2	3	2	8	1	4	..	..	2	2	2	..	..
4	2	..	1	43	22	20	18	45	26	27	23	27	5	15	9	12	1
5	1	..	..	11	5	6	3	13	8	5	1	16	5	5	7	18	3
6	..	1	..	13	9	6	2	16	6	11	6	12	6	5	5	14	4
7	..	..	..	1	..	..	1	1	1	..	..	2	..	1	..	..	..
8	..	..	..	..	..	..	..	..	..	..	..	1	..	..	..	2	..
9	..	..	..	..	..	..	..	..	..	..	..	..	..	..	..	..	..
10	..	..	..	..	..	..	..	..	..	..	..	..	..	..	..	..	..
Totals	5	1	2	73	39	35	27	78	42	47	30	59	18	28	23	42	8

No. of Rooms.	5½	5¾	6	6¼	6½	6¾	7	7¼	7½	7¾	8	8¼	8½	8¾	9	Totals.
1	..	..	..	..	..	..	..	..	..	..	..	..	..	..	..	..
2	..	..	..	..	..	..	..	..	..	..	..	..	..	..	..	8
3	1	1	..	..	..	..	..	..	..	..	..	..	..	..	..	27
4	7	10	3	2	..	1	1	1	..	..	..	..	..	..	..	321
5	3	3	3	2	..	..	1	3	1	..	..	1	2	..	..	121
6	2	6	6	1	2	3	4	2	..	1	3	..	..	1	1	148
7	..	..	..	..	..	..	..	..	1	..	..	..	..	..	..	8
8	..	..	..	..	..	..	..	..	..	1	..	..	..	..	1	5
9	..	..	..	..	..	..	1	..	..	..	..	..	..	..	..	..
10	..	..	..	..	..	..	..	..	..	..	..	..	..	..	..	1
Totals	13	20	12	5	2	4	7	6	2	2	3	1	2	1	2	639

rents were raised. The houses affected were mainly those with rentals of 3/6 to 4/6 a week, and the increase was in the majority of cases twopence or threepence, though in some cases it was 6d. and more.[1] According to one of the local newspapers, the *Warrington Guardian*, which published an article on " Rising Rents " in its

[1] There are now (April, 1914) very few houses at 3/6 in Warrington. What houses there are at this figure are mostly slum property which the Corporation is buying and demolishing as rapidly as possible. What houses there were at 4/- and 4/3 in September, 1913, are now 4/6 ; the latter are practically the lowest-rented houses distinct from slums.

issue of September 6, 1913, the increase affected considerably more than half of the cheaper class of dwellings. The rise is chiefly attributed by the *Guardian* representative to the dearth of working-class houses in the borough consequent upon the slackness in the building trade " during the past eighteen months." Other causes are said to be the demand for more elaborate repairs and the pressure of rates. It is further stated that tenants have not borne a fair share of this increase ; to quote an estate agent, " their children are being educated free, bowling greens have been provided and now they are to have tennis courts. Everything is being done for their benefit, and it is only equitable that they should help to pay for these schemes. Warrington is one of the lowest rented towns in the country in comparison with its rates."

Earners and Dependants

In Table II^w. (Appendix), p. 191, all the persons who fell within the scope of our enquiry are tabulated in two main divisions (wage-earners and non-wage-earners) and in subdivisions according to sex and age. It will be seen that 40 per cent. are wage-earners, a lower percentage than is to be found in Northampton. In fact per 100 households in Warrington there are 192 earners and 292 non-earners (compared with 203 and 227 in Northampton), and 115 school children and 61 children under five years (compared with 82 and 40 in Northampton).

In Warrington nearly 95 per cent. of all adult men and the great majority of youths and boys above school age are at work ; if not, the reason is generally illness or incapacity. Close upon three-quarters of the girls (over 14) and young women are in employment, while 8 per cent. of the married women and widows are wage earners. In addition to these a few married women supplement the family income with irregular earnings obtained by sewing, etc. Probably one of the most interesting features of the Table is the number of children under 14 who are at work (17 instances, out of which 5 are girls). These 17 children in our sample would probably represent 300 to 400 in the whole town. The regulation of the employment of young children is in the hands of the Local Education Authorities, who have the power at present to make their own by-laws and to enforce them after the sanction of the Board of Education has been received. At present the bye-laws of the Warrington Borough Council exempt a child from attending school if it is,

(1) between 12 and 14 years, and has reached the seventh standard ;

(2) between 13 and 14 years, and has obtained a certificate that it has made 350 attendances (after 5 years of age), in not more than two schools in each year for five years, whether consecutive or not.

Further, a child between 12 and 14 years is allowed to be employed " part-time," provided it has reached the fourth standard or made 300 attendances under the same conditions as stated above. It is needless to say that advantage is taken of these by-laws, especially by the poorer parents, with the result that we find such a large number of children who are really of school age in employment. Already other industrial centres have been taking action in the matter by raising the age limit for leaving school. It remains to be seen if Warrington will follow their example.

The number of children in the public elementary schools at the time of the enquiry was stated to be 13,518 (6,651 boys and 6,867 girls). Of these we should have in our sample 1 in 19·3, that is to say 700, less a few from shops. As a matter of fact we have about 35 more than this number—our sample being within the limits of probability as explained in chapter VI.

Returning to the 795 men and adult sons in the Table, it is found that 534 of them are heads of households, while 62 are lodgers, 79 live with their working mother or non-working parents and 120 work with their fathers or other men.

Table II^w (App., p. 191) is similar to the corresponding table for Northampton (Table II^N. Appendix) and only deals with individuals, not with households. But it is of interest to know also how the latter are constituted, and in Table IV. below the families are placed in certain groups according to the wage-earners and the number of dependent children.

One sees at a glance that in nearly half the families the man is the sole wage-earner, whilst he and one or more of his children are working in over a quarter of the families. In 3 per cent. of the households the wife is working, and in 4 per cent. women and children are the sole earners. In most cases it is economic pressure which has forced these women to seek employment, the cause frequently being the death or incapacity of the chief wage-earner, while in other cases his earnings are insufficient and have to be supplemented.

In 537 cases out of 640 the household is occupied by a man normally at work. Of the remaining 103 households, in 55 we found a " grown up " son in employment, through the parents either being ill or past work ; while a woman with no adult son is at the head of the house in 29 cases. Of the 19 households where there are no earners, 10 are those of old people with pensions or other means, 6 where widows or spinsters let apartments, 2 where the chief wage-earner is away but remits money to his wife, and in one there is no visible means of livelihood.

Referring to the statement in Chapter I., p. 31, it is found that there are at least 173 men out of 795 adult male wage-earners (*i.e.* 22 per cent.), who have to support a wife and two or more children, while it is possible

TABLE IV

EARNERS AND DEPENDENT CHILDREN

Man alone Earning.		Man and one or more Children Earning.		Man and Wife Earning.	
Dependent Children of all ages.	Number of Households.	Dependent Children of all ages.	Number of Households.	Dependent Children of all ages.	Number of Households.
0	62	0	41	0	—
1	66	1	32	1	4
2	57	2	33	2	8
3	60	3	23	3	3
4	32	4	23	4	2
5	14	5	12	5	2
6	6	6	11	6	1
7	4	—	—	—	—
	301		175		20[1]

Other cases where at least one Man over 20 years is working.		Women, Girls, and Lads under 20 Earning.		No Earnings.	
Dependent Children of all ages.	Number of Households.	Dependent Children of all ages.	Number of Households.	Dependent Children of all ages.	Number of Households.
0	52	0	14	0	13
1	20	1	4	1	3
2	10	2	6	2	1
3	9	3	2	3	2
4	4	4	1	—	—
5	0	5	2	—	—
6	1	—	—	—	.—
	96		29		19

[1] In 6 cases one or more children are also earning.

that some or all of 142 others (18 per cent.) have the same duty.

As was remarked in the previous chapter, the above classification of households does not give one any information as to the varying size of families. For this purpose one would have to study the more elaborate classification of households to be found in the App., p. 200 (Table III.ᵂ). This classification appears at first sight rather complex[1] but only a little explanation is required to make it quite easily understood. For instance, to take the first section, we see that there are 301 families where the man is the sole wage-earner. Out of these 301 families it is found that in 64 cases the man has no children dependent upon him. These 64 households can be further subdivided, for in 60 the man is married and his wife is living, in one the man has, in addition to his wife, an adult daughter, and in another case a wife and two " grown up " daughters. It is only in two cases out of the 64 that the man has no dependants at all. In the same way the rest of the Table should be read. It only remains to explain one other point, and that is the interpretation of " Working on their own account." There are 16 households classed under this heading; they are merely cases where the workers are in some small way of business—for instance, rag and bone men, salt hawkers, etc.

Of the facts that can be deduced from detailed study of the Table we may give prominence to one, that is, that in over 10 per cent. of the families,

---

[1] There are in all 304 different kinds of households in Warrington, and the family which is regarded by statisticians as being the normal one (man, wife and three dependent children) only occurs 55 times. As a matter of fact " the man, wife and two children " occur just as often as the latter, while " the man, wife and one child " appears to be the predominant type. This is found to be the case with Reading ; in Northampton, however, " man and wife " is the predominant type.

the children, young or adult, are the sole wage-
earners.

Earnings

The question of earnings is one of some difficulty even
in towns where time rates are in operation to a great
extent, but it becomes far more complex when piece-
work predominates. It is this payment by piece rates,
together with other difficulties arising out of the presence
of the iron trade in Warrington, which makes it difficult
even for official bodies to obtain reliable information.
Several local residents feared that in this respect the
enquiry would fail. That this has not been the case is
shown in the following pages. It is of interest, however,
to see what are the special difficulties which stood in
the way of procuring definite data as to earnings in this
town.

As mentioned above, the iron trade is largely responsible for the many complexities created. Not only is
payment chiefly made by the piece, but also the rates are
very numerous owing to the extensive sub-division of
employment. In addition, there is considerable variation
in the rate of remuneration of persons who at first sight
appear to carry out the same kind of work. To take an
example from the ironworks, a roller (and there are several
grades of rollers) is paid according to the size of the mill
or forge at which he is working ; if it happens to be an
11-inch mill an under-roller will earn, let us say, 5/6 a
day ; if a 14-inch mill, he will earn more, say 8/- to 10/-.
Then again, large numbers of ironworkers do not work
the full week, for when they are on piece-work they please
themselves as to how long they work. Frequently men
" knock off " when they have made a certain amount of
money. Much time is thus lost, particularly among the
puddlers at the forge, though this is not the case with men
working at the mill. The reason for the loss of time is

that the majority of puddlers are men advanced in years ; hence, owing to the excessive heat and exertion, they cannot stand a full week's work.[1] Further complexities arise through the difference in payment of day-shift men and night-shift men ; but as the men work day and night shifts alternately one can determine their average weekly wage from their fortnightly earnings. The existence of bi-turn men, however, tends to upset any calculations in this case on these lines.

Another difficulty has to be faced through work being let out on contract. This system of contracting is found to a considerable extent in the iron works. A " contractor " undertakes a " job," and for this purpose employs a number of undermen. He then receives payment for the work done by the whole " gang " and shares it among his men. The scale of payment to the undermen rests entirely upon arrangements between the undermen and the contractor, not on the employer, who deals only with the contractor. The employers, however, keep a full record of payments made to all persons directly or indirectly in the employment of the firm. This contract system leads to greater deviations from the average wage for various grades of labour than would be the case if standard rates of wages had been agreed upon by employers and employees. Nevertheless, certain recognised rates are in force. These were supplied by employers as well as by certain leading representatives of labour, and serve a useful purpose by checking those wage statements (for example, those of lodgers whose names were not known) where reference to the employers was impracticable.

[1] The average week of a puddler, on the authority of a well-known Trade Unionist connected with the Warrington iron trade, is between 3 and 4 shifts. The millmen and the men at the forge, other than puddlers, may be said to work about $4\frac{3}{4}$ days a week on the average. The days worked are not necessarily succeeding ones and as a result such irregularity is produced as has led to the creation of a class of bi-turn men who fill the places of any absentees.

These difficulties to a great extent disappeared through the co-operation of several employers who made wage returns for persons who figured in lists submitted to them, and thus enabled us to check the employees' statements. It was fortunate, too, that the returns made were for the most part those of persons whose wages were liable to great variations—that is, of persons engaged in the iron trade, in the broad sense of the term ; while it was mostly in those cases where the wage could be determined within narrow limits that the employers failed to reply. Taking the returns as a whole, the wages of two in every eleven of the wage-earners in Warrington were checked, and it was found that 60 per cent. were stated correctly within two shillings above or below. The great discrepancies (both under-statements and over-statements) in wage returns were found almost entirely to be in the case of iron workers (piece-workers). In some cases the discrepancies were due to or exaggerated by the fact that employers or employees included overtime in their returns. What is of importance is the fact, clearly shown from tabulating the discrepancies in relation to the amount of wages stated by the employee, that these differences were slight in the case of low wages (the greatest being 2/- in a wage of 22/-), whilst it was in the high wages that they were greatest. On the whole, it can hardly be supposed from the facts before us that there was any general tendency for a deliberate mis-statement to be made, though it is possible that this was so in a few cases. In the tabulation of families in their relative position to the standard, the employees' statements have been utilised, but in all cases where, according to the employers' statement, the family is *above* the standard, it has been placed above.

In addition to the one-fifth of our wage-earners as to whose earnings definite information was obtained, there was a large number of persons—labourers and certain other grades of male workers, but more particularly

H

women and children—whose wages could be fixed within narrow limits, and checked either in the light of statements made by employers or by standard or trade union rates. In 95 per cent. of the remaining cases the wages of the adult wage-earner were definitely stated; and assuming, as one may do, that the deviation from the truth of their statements was the same as found to be in those cases where checking was possible, it leaves us with only a very small percentage of cases where the information may be regarded as being unreliable. It should be noted, however, that in no case was a family placed below the poverty line if the wage statements were uncertain, or likely to be unreliable, or if the work was of such a nature as to result in earnings varying greatly in amount, as, for instance, in the case of a salt hawker.

In Table V. are to be found the employees' statements of the wages of adult males, separating the married householders from other wage-earners. Dealing with the former first, a very small percentage (only about 2) of these were found to be earning less than £1, about 36 per cent. earn less than 25/-, 70 per cent. less than 35/-, while about 14 per cent. earn more than £2—the average is approximately 28/6. Turning to the men over 20 other than householders, one would naturally expect to find them less highly paid. This proves to be so. About 7 per cent. earn less than £1 as compared with 2 per cent. in the case of married householders. The average wage is also lower, being about 25/6 as compared with 27/6. Moreover, the percentage of those who earn more than £2 a week is 5, as compared with 14 in the case of married householders. Other percentages can easily be worked out by the reader, and further comparisons drawn. Regarding the wages of all males over 20 as a whole, it is found that there were about 3½ per cent. earning less than £1 per week, about 11 per cent. more than £2 a week, and 86 per cent. be-

TABLE V

FULL TIME WAGES OF ADULT MALES. ALL TRADES

Normal Weekly Wage Rate.	Married Householders.			Other Men over 20 years, where known.	Total.
	Stated.	Estimated.	Together.		
NUMBER.	474	40	514	234	748
Unknown—					
Under 18/–	2	1	3	9	12
18/– to 19/–	5	..	5	6	11
19/– „ 20/–	2	..	2	2	4
20/– „ 21/–	43	5	48	21	69
21/– „ 22/–	29	1	30	11	41
22/– „ 23/–	22	1	23	23	46
23/– „ 24/–	26	3	29	24	53
24/– „ 25/–	45	..	45	15	60
25/– „ 26/–	35	1	36	29	65
26/– „ 27/–	14	2	16	8	24
27/– „ 28/–	18	..	18	6	24
28/– „ 29/–	36	4	40	10	50
29/– „ 30/–	3	1	4	—	4
30/– „ 31/–	34	4	38	18	56
31/– „ 35/–	36	1	37	14	51
35/– „ 40/–	61	7	68	26	94
40/– and over	63	9	72	12	84
Approximate Average	27/6	30/6	28/6	25/6	26/6

tween £1 and £2 (36 per cent. earning from 20/– to 25/–, 23 per cent. between 25/– and 30/–, and 27 per cent. between 30/– and £2).

In comparing these results with those obtained from the statements of employers, certain reservations have to be made. The employers who were asked to give information were all those whose workpeople figured largely in the returns. These would be nearly all persons in regular employment—no information was obtained for those who were their own masters or working for small firms—with the result that one would expect some of the lower paid wage-earners to be excluded. Again, though a number of firms kindly replied to our questions, and amongst them were several wire or iron works which employ a number of persons at relatively high wages, some did not, and it is possible that amongst the latter figured a few who paid low wages—that this was the case in one or two instances at least is without doubt. Further, one would naturally expect employees, if they were biassed in their statements at all, to understate rather than overstate their wages. These three factors operating at the same time would have the effect of producing a larger percentage at the higher end of the wage scale, and less at the lower end. Let us see to what extent this has been the case.

	Employees.	Employers.	Differences in percentages of statements of employees above (+) or below (—) employers.
Under £1..	3½ per cent.	2½ per cent.	+ 1
20/– to 25/–	36 ,,	21 ,,	+15
25/– ,, 30/–	22 ,,	24 ,,	+ 2
30/– ,, 35/–	14 ,,	19½ ,,	—5½
35/– ,, 40/–	13 ,,	15½ ,,	—2½
40/–and over	11 ,,	17 ,,	—6

It will readily be seen that the employers' returns have missed a large section between 20/- and 25/-, Warrington being a place where a great variety of work is carried out by labourers. Furthermore, the preponderance of the returns of firms engaged in the iron trade accounts for the excess at high wages.

We next come to the rates of wages paid in the chief industries of the town. The iron trade,[1] which employed over 7,500 persons in 1911, is by far the most important industry and calls for first attention.

Iron Trade.—In this industry are to be found a large number of men who, if they work full time, receive very high wages, £5 a week being not uncommon, while some receive as much as £10 or even £20 a week. But at the other end of the wage scale is a large class of persons, unskilled labourers, who for a full week of 53 hours receive £1 to 24/-.[2] When there is depression in the iron trade it is this class which suffers particularly heavily. During the latter period of this enquiry depression, consequent upon the prosperous times which the iron trade has experienced of recent years, set in, and many instances of families being placed in straitened circumstances came to the knowledge of our investigators. Families such as these would not be included in the number of those below the poverty line, unless they fell under it even when the wage-earner òr earners are working full time. That so many families are able to exist under these circumstances without seeking public charity is largely owing to the spirit of comradeship which exists amongst these classes. Not only do large numbers become " strap " customers (persons who buy on " tick "), but neighbours are often willing to help a family which is " down " through no fault of its own.

[1] Wire works and gas stove works are included under this heading.
[2] Since the enquiry was held the labourers at the ironworks have obtained a minimum wage of 22/1 per week.

It is extremely difficult to generalize in wage statements, even for different grades of labour, owing to the complexities mentioned on p. 111, but one can take it on reliable authority that an ironworker on piecework should get at least 30/- a week when fully employed. Furthermore, an attempt has been made to give the average full time weekly wage of various grades of ironworkers, based upon the statements of prominent labour representatives. Owing to the many reservations which have to be taken into account, these figures should be accepted with great caution :—

Forge Workers.	Average Weekly Wage.	Average Hours Worked.
Pig wheeler ..	(a) 45/- (b) 30/-	} 10½-hour day
Shingler	£3 to £5	11 ,, ,,
Forge roller ..	45/- to 50/-	11 ,, ,,
Roller's helper ..	22/6 to 30/-	11 ,, ,,
Puddler ..	(a) 50/- to 55/- (b) 30/- to 33/-	} 11 ,, ,,
Ball furnaceman ..	(a) £3 to £5 (b) 40/- to 44/-	} 11 ,, ,,
Barweigher ..	45/- to 50/-	11 ,, ,,

Mill Workers.	Average Weekly Wage.	Average Hours Worked.
Cutter-down ..	(a) £3 .. .. (b) 25/- to 35/-	} 10½ to 11-hour day.
(1) Wheeler ..	27/6 to 30/-	
(2) Piler	20/- to 35/- ..	
Furnaceman ..	(a) £3 to £5 .. (b) 27/6 to 40/- ..	} 12-hour day or more
Roller	£6 to £7	12-hour day.
Roller's helper ..	30/- to 55/- ..	12 ,,
(1) Bolter-down	£3	
(2) Catcher ..	About 30/- ..	} Same hours as Rollers.
(3) Hooker ..	12/6 to 27/6 ..	
(4) Sawyer ..	33/- to 36/- ..	
(5) Straightener	22/6 to 27/6 ..	

Those classed (b) are helpers to those classed (a).

Although the iron worker receives a comparatively high wage it must be borne in mind that his work is heavy and arduous, and that there are certain disadvantages and expenses attached to his occupation which are not incurred by persons engaged in trades where wages as a whole are lower. Not only do the puddlers and their assistants as well as furnacemen have to stand sweating before a blazing furnace, but the other workers also are constantly in proximity to excessive heat. Moreover, once the furnace is lit and the charge entered the puddler cannot leave his work. In fact he is usually uncertain when he will be leaving his work, and as a consequence irregularity of meal hours arises and frequently he is forced to take his food before he wants it. When it is not possible to return home for meals, the food is conveyed to the works and frequently consumed in a dried condition, caused by exposure in an atmosphere of high temperature. Sometimes, indeed, especially in summer, food is wasted through its getting too dry.

Moreover, the cost of living to an iron worker is higher than to the ordinary wage earner because of the very heavy wear of clothes and boots. This is partly caused through fire burns, etc. A prominent iron worker states that he requires three pairs of good stout 9/- boots in a year. Shirts also are a heavy item of expenditure, as they have to be flannel. Since the men are exposed to great variations in temperature cotton shirts would lead to chills and other illnesses.

A minor disadvantage of being employed in the iron trade is the fact that if a man wanted to attend evening classes in order to improve himself, he would be unable to do so owing to his having to work day and night shifts alternate weeks. This could probably be overcome by running two classes (tutored by the same person) to suit the convenience of both day and night-shift men—the same subject being taught at both classes. Many iron workers would then probably avail themselves of this opportunity.

Wire Trade.—A subdivision of the main industry is the wire trade, which is composed mainly of labourers and semi-skilled workers. The labourers in some of the wire factories receive a wage as low as 18/–, others 22/– or more. Next to them come the semi-skilled workers —machinists who receive anything from, say, 25/– to 30/– according to the job performed. The average wage received in the higher grades is about 35/–, though a few persons in responsible positions receive £5 or more.

The wages for the *Gas Stove Industry*, owing to the small number of firms engaged in it, will not be disclosed in detail. It is common knowledge, however, that, generally speaking, all grades with the exception of packers, japanners and enamellers, and labourers, receive 30/– a week or more. Labourers usually receive anything from 20/– to 25/–; while japanners and enamellers average about 25/–; however, some earn considerably above and below this.

STANDARD RATES OF WAGES. Oct. 1st, 1913.

Building Trades.	Rate of Wage	Summer Hours.
Bricklayers	9¾d. per hr.	54½ hours per week
Masons—		
(a) Banker hands ..	8¾ ,,	54½ ,, ,,
(b) Fixers	9¼d. ,,	54½ ,, ,,
Carpenters and Joiners ..	9½d. ,,	49½ ,, ,,
Plumbers	9½d. ,,	54½ ,, ,,
Plasterers	9½d. ,,	54½ ,, ,,
Painters	8½d. ,,	54½ & 55 hrs. per week
Labourers—		
Bricklayers'	6d. ,,	
Masons'	5½d. & 6d.	} 53 hours per week.
Plasterers'	6d. & 6½d.	

In point of the number of males employed, the *Building*

Trade comes next in importance after the Iron Industry. In 1911 there were 1,500 persons employed in this trade. The standard rates of wages are to be found in the Board of Trade Report on Standard Time Rates of Wages in the United Kingdom (Cd. 7194) and are appended below :—

Chemical and Soap Trade.—Two main groups of wage-earners are to be found in this trade. One group—the unskilled labourers—receive a minimum of 22/- (at the time of the enquiry an application was being made for an increase to 24/-), and rise to 25/- or 26/-. As a whole, this class of unskilled labourers is the best paid in the town. Then there is a very large number of men who work on the shift system. These men are employed for seven shifts of 8 hours each, and their earnings vary between 4/3 and 5/9 a shift. Finally there is a small class of skilled artisans who are paid on recognised standard rates. It may be said that working conditions in this trade compare very favourably with any other industry in the town.

Tanneries.—Payment for work in the Tanneries is mainly by piece rates, except in the case of tan-yard labourers, line jobbers and warehousemen, the two former being employed both at piece and time rates. All piece workers, with the exception of the tan-yard labourers who receive about 32/- on piecework and 24/- on day work, are paid at least 35/-, fleshers being the best paid.

Standard rates of wages in various occupations have been obtained from the Board of Trade Report (mentioned above) and are given below :—

Engineers.			Average Weekly Wage.	Hours of Labour.
(a) *General.*—Borers,	Slotters,			
Planers, Millers	..	..	36/-	53 hours.
Turners, Fitters,	Smiths			
and Millwrights	..	..	38/-	53 ,,
Pattern Makers ..	,,	,,	40/-	53 ,,

Engineers (continued).	Average Weekly Wage.	Hours of Labour.
(b) *Mills and Railway Shops.*—Turners, Fitters, Smiths and Millwrights	35/-	53 hrs.

Ironfoundry.

| Ironfounders .. .. .. | 42/- | 53, 54 hrs. |
| Patternmakers .. .. .. | 40/- | 53, 54 ,, |

Boilermakers.

Angle Iron Smiths..	43/-	
Platers	41/-	53 hrs.
Rivetters and Caulkers	37/-	
Holders up	34/-	

Printing, &c.

| Lithographic printing .. .. | 35/- | 47, 50 hrs. |
| Bookbinders and Machine Rulers .. | 30/- | 52 hrs |

Furnishing Trades.

Cabinet Makers, 9½d. per hour	
French Polishers, 8½d. per hour,	51 hours per week.
Upholsterers, 9d. per hour	

Gas Works.

Machine Stokers, 5/8 per day of 8 hours (Sundays 8/6).

Police.

Minimum, 28/-. Maximum, 36/-.

From other sources we have :—

Weekly Wage.

Railway Workers.

Platelayers	19/-.
Gangers	30/- to £2.
Porters..	15/- if under 19 years of age.
	17/6 at 19 years of age.
	21/- at 21 years of age.

Extra if they qualify for porter signalman and porter guard.

In addition tips vary from 2/- to 5/- a day.

Railway Workers (continued). Weekly Wage.

    Carters .. .. 25/- to 30/-.

    Engine Drivers .. Varies—some receive so much a week; some so much a journey, in which case the number of journeys is often restricted.

Earnings of Youths and Lads

So far we have been concerned with the earnings of adult males, but it is of importance also to know the average wage lads and youths receive. In the *Iron*

Age.	Iron Trade.	Tanneries.	Certain Factories.	Shops.
13 years 14 ,, 16 ,, 18 ,,	} 5/- to 9/- About 10/- 15/- or 16/- or piece- work.	5/- 6/- 10/- 14/- or piece-work	.. 6/- .. 16/-	4/- 5/- or 6/- About 10/- ..

Industry, in the broad sense of the term, lads from 13 to 15 years get about 5/- to 9/-, while at 16 they would average about 10/-; this latter appears to be the average wage of lads of this age in nearly all the important occupations in the town. A youth of 18 would receive about 15/- or 16/- if a time-worker, but probably considerably more if he was on piece-work.

A boy of 13 or 14 in a *Tannery* would probably get about 5/- for a start with a 2/- rise each year. He would receive this rate of increase until he commences piece-work —which may be at about 18 years of age.

In *Factories* he starts, as a rule, upon 6/– a week at the age of 14. The following year he would get 1/– rise, while at 18 years he would probably be earning 16/– a week.

The tabulation on the previous page brings these facts out more clearly.

The above are average wages—there is considerable variation in the case of youths and even, in a few cases, amongst boys. Frequently a youth of the age of 17, 18 or 19 is on piece-work earning much the same as an adult.

Earnings of Women and Girls

Women are employed largely in textile manufactures (including fustian cutting), domestic service, dressmaking and as soap workers. Owing to the small number of factories employing much women's labour, it would probably lead to their identification if the wages of persons were stated and the occupation to which these wages referred were named. Hence wages in various trades will be stated without any reference to the nature of the work carried out.

In one large factory girls of 13 or 14 years receive 6/– per week, or if they have passed the Seventh Standard they receive 7/–. At the age of 16 they would be getting 8/– to 10/–. Adult women have a wage of from 13/– to 15/–. The conditions of employment are good and much is done for the health of the workers.

In another factory, which draws upon a poorer class of worker, the girls of 13 and 14 have a commencing wage of 2/6 to 3/6, according to the nature of the work done. They are nearly all learners, helpers and assistants. The wages of the elder girls in some departments are extremely low compared with wages for similar kinds of work in other towns—a girl of 16 getting from about 6/– to 8/–. On the other hand, some of the adult women earn " good money," anything from 18/– to 30/–, but large numbers of them are under the disadvantage of having to work in a temperature of about 80° amidst the deafening noise of machinery.

Fustian or Velvet Cutting.—Owing to the number of firms engaged in this industry it is possible to deal with wages in detail and make such criticisms as apply to the trade generally. The chief feature of fustian cutting in this centre is that the industry is confined almost entirely to girls and young women—it is regarded as a temporary trade. This is shown by the Census Report on Occupations (Vol. IX. of 1911). There were in 1911 641 females employed as fustian cutters, and rather more than 40 per cent. of these were under 20 years ; while 65 per cent. were under 25 and about 80 per cent. were under 35. This results in lower wages being paid, as a whole, than are to be found in Congleton, the chief centre of the manufacture, where more adults are employed in the trade.

The work is, to a large extent, manual, but the trade is being revolutionised by the introduction of machinery, which produces five times as much as by hand. The change will prove beneficial to the cutter in two ways :—

(1) The hand cutter will become a machine minder, and will engage in less fatiguing work. At the present time the hand cutter's work results in her having to walk up and down a distance of four yards, and cover in the course of a day over twenty miles. Though the girls in many cases can sit down when tired or go out for food, yet the work is very trying, especially in summer. The strain will probably in future be mental rather than physical, as the machine results in a greater concentration of the mind and less physical exertion.

Hand cutters start upon 4/- and rise up to 24/-, but only expert cutters engaged on very special work receive this high wage. The average hand cutter when working full time may be said to earn about 12/-, and as age does not play much part in determining the wage, young girls are frequently found earning this sum.

(2) With work which demands greater skill, one would naturally expect higher wages, and this is so. The machine cutter gets 5/- at the age of 13 and 14 years, then after three months 7/- or 8/-, and after six months 9/-. The most efficient cutters get as high as 22/-, but the average is 14/- and 15/-. As machinery has only recently been introduced, these rates of wages can hardly be regarded as fixed. Even at this early stage of development they compare very favourably with the wages of hand cutters.

Attention should be drawn to certain other matters of interest in connection with this industry. Occasional " slips " are made when cutting, and where a girl makes more than eight holes in a piece, she is fined ½d. a hole. About one in six of the girls are fined; the fines in most cases are about 2d. per week, but in very careless cases fines run to 5d., 10d., and even more. This safeguards the employer, but in some cases works rather oppressively.

One of the chief disadvantages in connection with fustian cutting is that cutters have constantly to wait for work. It is to be hoped that this will be changed with the development of machine cutting. Machine production is undoubtedly going to improve the lot of the cutter, but before these better conditions have become general a stage will have to be passed which for a time will result in displacement of labour, as is always the case in a period of transition. Signs were visible that the genesis of this stage had been reached while the enquiry was being carried out, as many instances of cutters being unemployed came to our knowledge. However, Warrington has a wonderful way of developing new industries, and while on the one hand, there was talk of displacement of labour in fustian cutting, on the other hand, it became generally known that the establishment of a clothing factory was being contemplated by the Co-operative Wholesale Society. Whatever may be its temporary effects, the transition is undoubtedly going to lead to better conditions for the cutter.

It is of interest to note that there are still a fair number of domestic cutters, though the numbers employed are diminishing.

Domestic Service.—Domestic servants generally receive 2/6 and food at the age of 13 or 14. Girls of 17 years and upwards are paid anything from 5/- to 10/-. It is impossible to lay down any definite wage, as the terms of engagement vary considerably.

Family Income and Rent

Utilising the same definition of family income as in the previous chapter, Table VI. was prepared. The tabulation not only shows the distribution of family income, but its relationship to the rent paid. A comparison of the distribution with the corresponding figures for Northampton (p. 77) shows that a larger ratio (over one-third) of Warrington families have an income of less than 30/-; while the percentage of families with over £3 a week is much the same in the two towns, namely 16½ per cent. in Northampton, 15 per cent. in Warrington. Nearly half the families in the latter town have an income of less than 35/-, and about 60 per cent. an income of less than £2—this leaves about a quarter with an income of between £2 and £3 a week.

It is found that all the three cases where the family income is less than 10/- and the rent is nil, are households where lodgers are kept—or rather are instances of single women keeping lodgers. Actually, the rent is not nil, but the lodgers' contributions to it cover the whole

TABLE VI

FAMILY INCOME AND RENT

Weekly Rent (including rates and allowing for lodgers).	FAMILY INCOME.						
	Under 10/-	10/- and under 15/-	15/- and under 20/-	20/- and under 25/-	25/- and under 30/-	30/- and under 35/-	35/- and under 40/-
0/- to 1/- ...	3	...	...	...	...	...	...
1/- „ 1/9 ...	2	...	...	1	2	1	1
2/- „ 2/9 ...	2	1	2	6	8	1	...
3/- „ 3/9 ...	3	2	5	33	18	10	7
4/- „ 4/9 ...	4	1	4	64	50	36	27
5/- „ 5/9 ...	...	1	...	6	14	22	19
6/- „ 6/9 ...	...	...	...	1	4	3	14
7/- „ 7/9 ...	...	...	...	...	...	...	3
8/- „ 8/9 ...	...	...	...	...	...	...	...
9/- „ 9/9 ...	...	...	...	...	...	1	...
10/- „ 10/9 ...	...	...	...	...	...	...	...
Totals	14	5	11	111	96	74	71
Median income ...	7/3	10/-	18/-	22/-	27/-	32/-	37/-
Median rent ...	2/10½	3/9	3/6	4/-	4/3	4/6	5/-
Rent as percentage of income ...	40	37½	19	18	16	14	13½

Weekly Rent (including rates and allowing for lodgers).	40/- and under 45/-	45/- and under 50/-	50/- and under 55/-	55/- and under 60/-	60/- and over.	Unknown.	Total.
0/- to 1/- ...	...	...	1	...	...	2	6
1/- „ 1/9 ...	...	...	...	...	1	...	8
2/- „ 2/9 ...	...	1	2	...	1	...	24
3/- „ 3/9 ...	6	1	1	5	6	3	100
4/- „ 4/9 ...	20	16	8	5	31	4	270
5/- „ 5/9 ...	10	16	5	4	27	2	126
6/- „ 6/9 ...	5	8	5	4	16	3	63
7/- „ 7/9 ...	5	3	1	4	11	2	29
8/- „ 8/9 ...	2	...	2	...	2	1	8
9/- „ 9/9 ...	1	...	1	...	...	...	2
10/- „ 10/9 ...	...	...	...	...	1	2	3
Totals	49	45	26	22	96	19	639
Median income ...	42/-	46/6	50/-	57/-	72/6	...	...
Median rent ...	4/9	5/-	5/-	5/-	5/1	...	...
Rent as percentage of income ...	11	11	10	9	7	...	...

amount in each case, and thus it is assumed that the woman lives rent free.

Family Income and the Poverty Line

Before the families in our sample can be placed in relation to the Minimum Standard or Poverty Line, the latter has to be established. It would not be possible to apply to Warrington the standard used for Northampton, unless the general prices of commodities consumed by the working classes in the two towns were found to be the same or much the same. We have, then, first of all, to draw a comparison between general prices in the two centres. We can do this in part from data collected at the time of the enquiries from co-operative stores and from shops who could furnish us with reliable records, but largely from the relative height of prices published in the Report of the Board of Trade Enquiry into the Cost of Living. The Government return gives the following index numbers :—

		Meat.	Other Food.	Total Food.	Coal.	Food and Coal.
Northampton	..	97	98	98	82	96
Warrington	..	91	99	97	74	94

Though food prices are only very slightly lower than in Northampton, coal prices are considerably lower in Warrington, which is not surprising, as it is situated on the fringe of the South Lancashire coalfield and within sight of pitshafts. But if the *amounts* of commodities consumed are taken into account, together with their prices, little difference exists. That it is essential to consider the amount is shown in the case of coal, which is consumed to a greater extent in Lancashire than in Northampton. After a careful study of the data, the conclusion arrived at is that the standard for Northampton may be regarded as being equally applicable to Warrington. Hence we proceed in the same way as in the last chapter to determine how many families are below and above this standard.

There are (Table IV.^W, App. p. 212), 74 families which fall below the New Standard, and 78 families below the Rowntree Standard, and 70 below both. In addition to

I

these there are 8 probably below both, making in all 82 and 86 respectively.[1] That is to say, $11\frac{1}{2}$ to $13\frac{1}{2}$ per cent. of the working-class families in Warrington, in so far as they are dependent on earnings, pensions, etc., are below the level necessary to keep them in physical health, except at the sacrifice of clothing and other necessary intermittent expenditure. As remarked in the previous chapter, this does not necessarily mean that there is $11\frac{1}{2}$ to $13\frac{1}{2}$ per cent. of the working-class families in distress, for it is possible that through presents, charity and poor relief some are able to live above the standard. On the other hand, there are a number of cases in which the data are insufficient to enable one to place the family definitely in its position with reference to the poverty line, and these are placed above and classed as doubtful. Moreover, the income of the families has been based on full time employment—that short time is frequent needs no proof.

In Table IV.[W], App., p. 212, the households are classified according to wage-earners and number of dependent children, but with special reference to those families definitely, probably or possibly below the standard. If the 537 households headed by an adult male wage-earner are considered, it is found that 72, or $13\frac{1}{2}$ per cent., are below one or both standards. This percentage rises to $29\frac{1}{2}$ in the case of those 173 households where a sole male wage-earner has two or more children dependent on him, which shows that not only do more families fall below as the number of dependants increases, but also that more children can be supported as the number of wage-earners increases.

As in Northampton, the bulk of the families below the

[1] Since the enquiry was made the labourers at the iron works have received a minimum wage of 22/1. The establishment of this minimum has resulted in three of the families below both standards and one more below the New Standard being raised above. The effect of this is to alter the percentage very slightly —11 to 13 per cent.

standard are those where a married man is the sole wage-earner. A very large percentage of families with the husband alone earning and the wife, together with four or more children, dependent upon him, fall below the poverty line. As soon as the children grow up and are able to work, the position of the family improves, as is shown by the following facts deduced from the Table IV.[W] :—

Where man alone is at work, 1 family in 6 is below standard.

Where man and 1 son or daughter are at work, 1 family in 8 is below standard.

Where man and 2 sons or daughters are at work, 1 family in 11 is below standard.

Where man and 3 sons or daughters are at work, 1 family in 27 is below standard.

In about 10 per cent. of the families below the poverty line, the husband is either dead or unable to work, and his widow or wife and children are forced to do so.

If we analyse the constitution of the households below the two standards, we find that they are composed as shown in Table VII. on the next page.

It is of interest to know the occupations of the chief wage-earners in households below the standard. About two-thirds of them are labourers, while 10 per cent. of them are carters. As was seen above, the establishment of the minimum wage of 22/1 for the labourers in the ironworks has had but little effect in raising the former above the poverty line. The occupations include a postman, and a bar weigher at one of the ironworks, but in both these cases the size of the families has been the cause of their falling below the standard.

This brings us to the causes of the deficiency in the income of these families. As we remarked in the previous chapter, it is extremely difficult to draw a definite line

TABLE VII

	EARNING.						
	Men over 20.	Women over 16.	Girls 14–16.	Sons 18–20.	Lads & Boys. 14–18.	School Children. 5–14.	Total.
Below New Standard	66	16	9	4	8	2	105
Total	844	211	46	59	49	17	1226
Percentage below	8	7½	19½	7	16	12	8¾

	DEPENDENT.						
	Men. over 18.	Women.	Girls.	Lads & Boys.	School Children.	Infants.	Total.
Below New Standard	5	73	2	1	181	88	350
Total	43	678	12	4	735	391	1863
Percentage below	11½	11	16½	..	24½	22½	19

	EARNING AND DEPENDENT.				
	Men.	Women.	Girls, Lads and Boys over 14.	Children and Infants under 14.	All.
Percentage below	8	10	14	23½	14.7

Persons below, 455 ; persons above, 2,634 ; total, 3,089.

of demarcation, because in some cases more than one factor is operating. In cases of doubt the cause which appears to be the chief one has been regarded as the only one. The results of the classification on these lines were given in Chapter I., p. 40.

It will be seen, then, that in exactly three-fifths of the cases low wages are the chief cause of the poverty of these families, whilst the size of the family accounts for a quarter. The death or incapacity of the chief wage-earner does not figure so largely as in the case of Northampton. It is, then, the low wages of the labouring class as a whole in Warrington, which is the root evil of the poverty in that town.

If the households below the standards are classified according to the wards in which they are situated, one finds again that the old portions of the borough are by far the worst. In both St. John's and Howley Wards 16 per cent. of the working-class houses contain families which do not have the minimum income necessary for their health. Latchford, on the other hand, is in a far more favourable position.

The wards are given below classified according to the extent of poverty in each :—

TABLE VIII

Ward.	No. of houses of all classes in sample.	No. of houses below the standard.	Proportion of houses below the standard.
Town Hall	41	4	1 in 10
Bewsey ..	50	3	1 in 17
Whitecross	87	8	1 in 11
Orford ..	89	11	1 in 8
St. John's	101	16	1 in 6
Fairfield ..	94	9	1 in 10½
Howley ..	55	9	1 in 6
St. Austin's	53	5	1 in 10½
Latchford	104	5	1 in 21
	674	70	—

Table IX. shows the distribution of families according to the amount their incomes differ from the two standards.

TABLE IX

FAMILIES ABOVE AND BELOW THE POVERTY LINE

RELATION TO MR. ROWNTREE'S STANDARD.				RELATION TO NEW STANDARD.			
Above.	No. of Households.	Below.	No. of Households.	Above.	No. of Households.	Below.	No. of Households.
Shillings.		Shillings.		Shillings.		Shillings.	
+40 & over	61	−13 ,, 14	1	+40 & over	59	−11 ,, 12	1
+35 to 40	21	−12 ,, 13	..	+35 to 40	17	−10 ,, 11	2
+30 ,, 35	21	−11 ,, 12	2	+30 ,, 35	18	−9 ,, 10	..
+25 ,, 30	34	−10 ,, 11	3	+25 ,, 30	34	−8 ,, 9	2
+20 ,, 25	50	−9 ,, 10	3	+20 ,, 25	50	−7 ,, 8	4
+18 ,, 20	29	−8 ,, 9	2	+18 ,, 20	22	−6 ,, 7	5
+16 ,, 18	23	−7 ,, 8	4	+16 ,, 18	31	−5 ,, 6	8
+14 ,, 16	31	−6 ,, 7	4	+14 ,, 16	32	−4 ,, 5	4
+12 ,, 14	31	−5 ,, 6	9	+12 ,, 14	30	−3 ,, 4	13
+10 ,, 12	37	−4 ,, 5	6	+10 ,, 12	37	−2 ,, 3	12
+8 ,, 10	42	−3 ,, 4	11	+8 ,, 10	48	−1 ,, 2	14
+7 ,, 8	14	−2 ,, 3	14	+7 ,, 8	16	−0 ,, 1	6
+6 ,, 7	26	−1 ,, 2	8	+6 ,, 7	23	Amount not known	3
+5 ,, 6	13	−0 ,, 1	8	+5 ,, 6	16		
+4 ,, 5	17	Amount not known	3	+4 ,, 5	22		
+3 ,, 4	13			+3 ,, 4	15		
+2 ,, 3	27			+2 ,, 3	25		
+1 ,, 2	17			+1 ,, 2	19		
+0 ,, 1	14			+0 ,, 1	11		
Amount not known	28			Amount not known	28		
	549		**78**		**553**		**74**
		On line	.. .. ..	4			
		Possibly below ..	.. .. ..	1	} 13		
		Probably below ..	.. .. ..	8			

Budgets

Some difficulty was experienced in getting families to keep budgets. Only two were sufficiently well kept to be published. These are summarised below and relate to two families which, for the purpose of convenience, we will call A and B.

Family A is composed of a widow aged 56, with two daughters (25 and 23 years). The two girls are both in employment in a factory, while the widow herself cleans offices. The total earnings average 27/6. The house in which they live is a four-roomed one with a small garden. In the Table below relating to this family certain items need explanation. Clothing is bought thus : 2/- a week is paid into two clothing clubs, *i.e.*, 1/- to each club. The clubs run for 20 weeks, and each person is entitled to draw 20/- at some time or other. At the beginning of each period lots are drawn to decide in what order the members shall draw the money. Twenty people pay in a total of 20/- weekly and 20/- is drawn out by one member according to lot drawn. Two shillings per week all the year round is not enough to pay all clothing expenses apart from boots. In seven weeks 2/9 has been paid for material in addition. The girls make their own blouses. Boots are similarly paid for, except that money is paid direct to a bootshop at the rate of 1/6 per week for the three in family. Boots and shoes are selected as required. This too is insufficient for all foot-wear; 4½d. was paid for a small repair during seven weeks, and it might have happened that more was needed. Both clothing and boot expenditures are fair samples of expenditure during the whole year. Coal is bought in fairly regular quantities—sometimes a little in excess of current requirements. Small accumulations make a little stock for a possible rainy day. It is a form of banking.

Food expenditure may be sub-divided as follows :—

Butcher (including bacon)	..	..	..	1/3
Baker, *i.e.*, flour and yeast	..	..	..	1/10
Milkman	..	..	..	..	1/7
Fishmonger	..	..	..	..	½
Vegetables and fruit		..	..	..	1/4½
Groceries	..	..	..	..	7/9
					13/10

The family bake their own bread from flour and hence bread does not figure in the baker's bill. Fish is scarcely bought at all, as they " do not care for it," possibly because the family do not care to be classed with the patrons of the fried fish shop.

The 7/9 spent in groceries includes 6d. a week, which is paid weekly into a Christmas Club—the value is taken out in groceries during the festive season. The family buy about 5/- of their groceries every week from the Co-operative Stores and receive a dividend periodically upon purchases made there. Discretion is used in buying groceries, etc., and purchases are made elsewhere if there seems to be any advantage. Real intelligence is used in the purchase of such things as tea and butter. It is known how long half a pound of butter from different shops will last. Quality is also studied carefully.

Family B is composed of man aged 29, wife aged 36, and children aged 9, 7 and 4½ years. The man is in regular unskilled work, employed daily, but professedly not for full days. His standing wage is 17/6, but he frequently earns much more owing to pressure of work, or through taking the place of men absent through sickness. During the slack times he earns extra money in the evenings in several kinds of odd jobs. He is a handy and willing man. He kept no record of earnings when he was recording his expenditure. The account here set forth represents the expenditure made by the wife on the household from what money he could conveniently give her. Besides the items mentioned, the children have pennies given to them occasionally. The man never knows what his next week's earnings will be except that 17/6 is certain. He banks whenever possible anything up to 3/- a week. Out of money so saved clothes or other necessaries would be purchased.

	A.		B.	
	Actual Expenditure.	New Standard.	Actual Expenditure.	New Standard.
Rent	3/3	3/6	5/9	3/6
Clothes	3/11	1/6	—	2/3
Fuel and State Insurance ..	3/10	1/7	2/10	1/7
Food	13/10	11/0	12/4	14/2
Other expenditure	2/5½	6d.	1/–	10d.
	27/3½	18/1	21/11	22/4
Average Income	27/6	—	—	—

The Money-Lending Evil

Before closing this chapter a word should be said about an evil which social workers and all who have the interests of the wage-earning classes in Warrington at heart are endeavouring to combat. " Money-Lending Vampires," for this is the heading of an article which appeared in the *Warrington Examiner* dealing with the evil, stand outside the works and tempt the men to borrow. Cases are known where " men, working at the same job, earning the same pay, are in vastly different circumstances. One will have saved enough to be practically independent ; he has abstained from borrowing. His neighbour has not a shirt to his back : he has parted with his substance at the expense of the comfort of his household. The money is borrowed for drink or betting, but the result is the same—that in many cases a man's whole week's wages are mortgaged before he draws them, and every succeeding week his home expenses have to be run upon borrowings. . . . The sums lent are on the security of the promise to repay when the weekly wage is received. It may be lent any time during the week, even on the Friday night, but must be repaid with interest on pay day. The interest charged is worked upon the shilling, and is generally threepence—at the rate of 25 per cent. weekly, or 1,300 per cent. per annum. Through competition the rate has in some instances come down to twopence in the shilling." Though the persons who carry on this pernicious trade are despicable, yet the whole blame cannot be thrown upon them. The borrower through his weakness injures not only himself but his family and the community. " It is this man's children who need to be school fed, this man's child who requires clogs, this man's house that becomes a slum, this man's family that has to be publicly fed, when any difficulty arises, the result of temporary stoppage of work, as in the recent coal strike. This is the man who rears a family of underfed children, whose stunted brains and impoverished constitutions augment the number of the unemployable and cause the main drain on the resources of trade unions, thrift societies, and of the National Insurance Fund. This is the man who often finishes in the workhouse. Upon the community is thrown the ultimate results of much of the money lending, and it is the public who in their own interest, if for nothing else, ought and can alone stamp it out. Public opinion can do more than law."

CHAPTER IV

STANLEY

THE urban district of Stanley is 7 miles S.S.W. of New-castle-upon-Tyne, and 8 miles N.N.W. of Durham. It is situated in the heart of the Durham coalfield, and is well known through the appalling mining disaster which took place in one of the pits in 1909. Its inhabitants are engaged almost entirely in mining, no other industry, with, perhaps, the exception of agriculture and building, being at all conspicuous there. Its extraordinary recent growth has been consequent upon the development of its mineral resources.

The enquiry at Stanley was superintended and carried out in July, 1913, almost entirely by local residents. The method of selecting the houses to be investigated was similar to that in the other towns, except that, as there was no local directory, the burgess roll was utilised. The roll, however, does not include persons in receipt of poor relief ; hence a random selection of one in twenty of the latter was made.

Of the 242 houses selected it was found that 13 were shops, while 20 were those of principal residents, owner-ship voters, etc. The remaining 209 were visited by investigators, but the occupiers of 5 of these were subse-quently found not to belong to the working class (clerks, shop managers, etc.). The Tables in this chapter deal with these 204 working-class households, though in the case of one family the investigators failed to obtain any information.

As official returns relating to Stanley are few in number,

we cannot draw so many interesting comparisons between
our results and official figures as in the case of the other
towns surveyed. It is possible, however, to make comparisons with regard to overcrowding, and also to quote
extracts from official reports on subjects outside the scope
of this enquiry.

The Census Report (Vol. VI.) supplies information
relating to the population of the urban district in 1911
as follows :—

	Number.	Population.
Inhabited dwellings, houses, flats, etc.	3,889	22,773
Empty	33	—
Inhabited shops	49	268
Hotels, etc., offices, workshops, etc., and miscellaneous	27	185
Institutions	1	22
Uninhabited buildings	4	—
	4,003	23,294[1]

The multiplier to be applied to our sample is found to
be 17.

Housing

Housing conditions in Stanley are entirely different
from those in the other two towns. This arises from the
fact that the colliery companies provide houses free to a
number of their employees—the house in many cases
being of insufficient size to accommodate the family.
According to the Conciliation Board Arrangement,
November 5, 1900, it was resolved that " married workmen of the following classes and widowers of the same

[1] This total includes 46 persons in sheds, vagrants, etc.

classes having families, shall be allowed free houses or the customary allowance for rent in lieu thereof :—

Underground.—

Deputies.	Rolleywaymen.
Hewers.	Horsekeepers.
Stonemen.	Shot firers.
Shaftsmen.	Wastemen.
Timber drawers.	Shifters.
Onsetters.	

Aboveground.

Banksmen.

(Fillers have also been included in the above list since 1904, and Firemen since 1908.)

Further that " no rent allowance be granted to any person who is offered a colliery house and refuses to accept it."

The latter resolution is, no doubt, one of the factors which create over-crowding in colliery houses, and we shall presently see the effect it has in actual practice.

Workmen entitled to rent allowance receive it only if they are householders—the rent book has almost invariably to be shown before any allowance is made.

Close upon a third of the houses are owned by the collieries and are granted rent free to the above-named classes of employees. They are for the most part two-roomed or three-roomed, although there are also a number of four-roomed houses. The two-roomed houses consist of a bedroom and kitchen. The three-roomed house has an additional bedroom. It was found that half the two-roomed and a third of the three-roomed colliery houses were overcrowded (that is, according to the Census definition of overcrowding as more than two persons to one room). Several cases were found where as many as six or seven persons were inhabiting two rooms. That this state of affairs should be allowed to exist is scandalous.

Of the houses which are rented, the majority are three-roomed and four-roomed, although there are a small number with two rooms. The rents of the three–roomed houses are generally 5/6 and of the four-roomed 6/–; but it must be remembered that towards this certain grades of miners who are also householders receive an allowance usually of 3/–, though in some cases it is 2/9 and 2/6.

TABLE I

NUMBER OF WORKING-CLASS HOUSES CLASSIFIED ACCORDING TO RENTS AND ROOMS

Weekly Rent (including Rates).	NUMBER OF ROOMS									
	1	2	3	4	5	6	7	8	Unknown	Total.
Colliery House (free) ..	..	23	20	16	2	1	..	1	..	63
1/– to 1/9 ..	..	..	..	..	..	..	..	..	..	..
2/– ,, 2/9 ..	1	..	..	..	..	..	..	..	..	1
3/– ,, 3/9 ..	2	1	1	1	1	..	..	..	..	6
4/– ,, 4/9 ..	1	3	..	..	..	..	..	..	..	4
5/– ,, 5/9 ..	..	12	36	9	..	..	..	..	..	57
6/– ,, 6/9 ..	..	..	23	27	2	..	..	..	1	53
7/– ,, 7/9 ..	..	..	1	8	1	..	..	..	..	10
8/– ,, 8/9 ..	..	..	..	..	1	2	..	..	..	3
9 – ,, 9/9 ..	..	..	..	..	..	1	..	..	..	1
10/– ,, 10/9 ..	..	..	..	..	..	..	..	..	..	0
11/– ,, 11/9 ..	..	..	..	..	..	1	..	..	..	1
12/– ,, 12/9 ..	..	..	..	..	..	..	..	..	..	0
Own house .. (rent unknown)	..	..	..	2	..	1	..	..	..	3
Total	4	39	81	63	7	6	..	1	1	202
Median rent ..	3/3	5/–	5/6	6/3	6/6	9/–	..	..	..	..

In Table II. the number of persons in a household is shown in relation to the number of rooms. It is seen that there are 35 cases where, according to the Census definition, there is overcrowding, while in 26 other cases, shown in heavy type, there are exactly two persons to a room. In other words, 17 per cent. of the houses surveyed were found to be overcrowded. The percentage of overcrowding found by the Census authorities was 34, but this figure, it must be remembered, relates to 1911, and since that date the district council have been issuing closing orders against several streets of colliery houses, while new houses with more rooms have been built. In 1913 alone 102 new houses were erected, but according to the report of the Medical Officer of Health, 1913, " private enterprise has not during the year supplied the demand for houses for the working classes, and consequently there is overcrowding to some extent throughout the whole district." Of the 102 new houses erected, 94 were self-contained and 8 were tenements, the latter having three rooms and a scullery downstairs, and four rooms with a scullery upstairs, with self-contained yards. Of the self-contained houses 28 contained two rooms and a scullery, 44 contained four rooms and a scullery, 15 contained five rooms and a scullery.

TABLE II

NUMBER OF WORKING-CLASS HOUSES CLASSIFIED ACCORD-
ING TO THE NUMBER OF PERSONS AND OF ROOMS

Number of Rooms.	NUMBER OF PERSONS.													Total.
	1	2	3	4	5	6	7	8	9	10	11	12	13	
1	..	2	2	..	..	..	..	..	..	..	..	..	..	4
2	1	3	12	8	4	5	5	1	..	..	..	..	..	39
3	..	6	26	15	17	5	5	1	4	2	..	1	..	82
4	..	9	12	6	7	3	12	10	2	2	..	..	..	63
5	..	1	3	1	..	..	1	..	..	..	..	..	1	7
6	..	..	1	1	..	1	..	2	..	..	..	1	..	6
8	..	..	..	..	..	..	..	..	..	..	..	1	..	1
Unknown ..	..	..	..	1	..	..	..	..	..	..	..	..	..	1
Total ..	1	21	56	32	28	14	23	14	6	4	..	3	1	203

TABLE III

NUMBER OF WORKING-CLASS HOUSES CLASSIFIED ACCORDING TO THE NUMBER OF EQUIVALENT ADULTS AND OF ROOMS

No. of Rooms.	NUMBER OF EQUIVALENT ADULTS IN HOUSES.														
	1	1¼	1½	1¾	2	2¼	2½	2¾	3	3¼	3½	3¾	4	4¼	4½
1	..	..	..	..	2	1	1	..	..	..	..	..	..	..	..
2	1	..	..	..	8	6	4	6	4	2	..	..	4	1	3
3	..	..	..	1	6	11	8	12	11	3	4	3	4	2	2
4	..	..	..	..	9	5	2	5	6	2	2	..	2	2	1
5	..	..	..	..	1	3	..	..	..	1	..	..	..	..	..
6	..	..	..	..	..	..	..	..	1	..	..	..	1	..	..
Unknown	..	..	..	..	..	..	1	..	..	..	..	..	..	..	..
Total	1	..	..	1	21	26	16	23	22	8	6	3	11	5	6

No. of Rooms.	4¾	5	5¼	5½	5¾	6	6¼	6½	6¾	7	7¼	7½	7¾	8	8¼
1	..	..	..	..	..	..	..	..	..	..	..	..	..	..	..
2	..	2	..	..	..	..	..	..	..	..	..	..	..	..	..
3	2	2	3	2	2	..	..	2	..	..	..	..	1	..	..
4	3	4	1	2	2	1	..	3	4	..	2	..	2	..	1
5	..	..	..	..	..	..	..	..	1	..	..	..	..	..	..
6	..	..	..	..	..	1	..	1	1	..	..	..	..	..	..
Unknown	..	..	..	..	..	..	..	..	..	..	..	..	..	..	..
Total	5	8	4	4	4	2	..	6	6	..	2	..	3	..	1

No. of Rooms.	8½	8¾	9	9¼	9½	9¾	10	10¼	10½	10¾	11	11¼	Totals.
1	..	..	..	..	..	..	..	..	..	..	..	..	4
2	..	..	..	..	..	..	..	..	..	..	..	..	36
3	..	..	..	..	..	..	..	..	..	..	..	..	81
4	..	..	..	..	..	..	..	..	..	..	..	..	61
5	..	..	..	..	1	..	..	..	..	..	..	..	7
6	..	..	..	..	..	..	..	1	..	..	..	..	6
8	..	..	..	..	..	..	..	..	..	..	..	1	1
Total	..	..	..	..	1	..	..	1	..	..	..	1	196
													Unknown 1
													No data 1
													198

Of the 35 households where overcrowding existed at the time of our enquiry, over half were families residing in colliery houses, though the latter form only one-third of the houses in Stanley which are occupied by wage-earners.

Obviously, therefore, it is in connection with the colliery house that the evil of overcrowding is most serious.

Measured by the more elastic test, overcrowding is found to exist in 50 per cent. of the houses. It is most prevalent in two and three-roomed houses ; indeed, in only 4 out of 36 two-roomed houses is there sufficient room, while over one-third of the three-roomed houses are overcrowded. It can hardly be doubted that the existence of overcrowding on so serious a scale is one of the chief factors which give rise to such a high infantile mortality as is found in Stanley, *viz.*, 169 per 1,000 births.

In the Appendix, p. 189, is placed Table I.², showing the accommodation of certain typical houses.

Earners and Dependants

It will be seen from Table II². (App., p. 192) that the 204 houses, which form the subject of our study, contained 975 persons, of whom 329 were earners and 646 not. The large percentage of men who are not at work compared with other towns is occasioned by the fact that in Stanley a great number are disabled and invalided through mining accidents. Another striking feature of the Table is that the percentage of women at work is very small. There is no demand for women's labour, and the few who are employed are mostly charwomen, whilst the girls and young women are dressmakers, or are employed in shops or in picture palaces as pianists and ticket collectors. The total number of school children in Stanley during July, 1913, was 4,315.[1] The number of children under 14 years per 100 houses is very nearly the same as at Warrington (p. 106.) Practically all the able-bodied men and boys over 16 years are at work.

[1] The number, therefore, which should appear in our returns is 248, less children from shops, etc. The number actually appearing in them is 214.

K

TABLE IV

EARNERS AND DEPENDENT CHILDREN

MAN ONLY EARNING.		MAN AND ONE OR MORE CHILDREN EARNING.		MAN AND WIFE EARNING.[1]	
Dependent Children of all Ages.	Number of Households.	Dependent Children of all Ages.	Number of Households.	Dependent Children of all Ages.	Number of Households.
0	21	0	7	0	1
1	38	1	4	..	..
2	24	2	9	2	1
3	21	3	8	..	..
4	5	4	5	..	..
5	8	5	8	..	..
6	2	6	2	..	..
7	1	7	1	..	..
	120		44		2

OTHER CASES WHERE AT LEAST ONE MAN OVER 20 YEARS IS WORKING.		WOMEN, GIRLS, AND LADS UNDER 20 EARNING.		NO EARNINGS.	
Dependent Children of all Ages.	Number of Households.	Dependent Children of all Ages.	Number of Households.	Dependent Children of all Ages,	Number of Households.
0	5	0	1	0	5
1	3	1	1	1	2
2	5	2	2	2	2
3	2	4	2	3	1
4	1	5	1	4	1
6	1	6	1	5	1
	17		8		12

The classification of the households given in Table IV. shows that in well over half of the cases (60 per cent., in fact) the family has only one wage-earner—an adult male. In only one case are a man and his wife at work. From the classification as given in Table IV. and in Table

[1] In one of the two cases here it is " woman " instead of " wife."

IV*., App., p. 216, it is found that in 172 cases the house is occupied by an adult male at work.· Of the remaining cases, in 11 at least one adult son is at work, with parents unable to work through age or illness ; in 8 others a woman is at the head of the house ; in 6 cases the occupier is past work ; in 6 cases there are no apparent means of livelihood—two of these cases are women keeping lodgers, where the male wage-earners have for a considerable time been incapacitated through phthisis and cardiac debility respectively, while another case is of a widow whose husband was killed in the mine.

Of the 259 men and adult sons found in Table II*. (Appendix), 172 are the heads of households, 25 are lodgers, 17 live with their working mother or non-working parents, and 45 work with their fathers or other men.

With reference to the statement in Chapter I., p. 31, concerning assertions made in minimum wage discussions, Stanley shows that the number of adult men who have to support a wife and two or more children is at least 61 out of the 259 (24 per cent.), whereas it may be as many as 104 (40 per cent.).

Earnings

As coal mining is almost the only occupation of any size in which the inhabitants of Stanley are engaged, rates of wages will only be given for the various grades of labour employed in this industry.

As the investigation was carried out by persons who were fully acquainted with mining and with the rates of payment and conditions of employment in the several pits, they were able to verify then and there the statements of persons interrogated. The statements were further checked in the light of the Minimum Wage Agreement. Hence it was considered unnecessary to make any reference to employers.

In the following schedule are given the Minimum Wages and the Hours of Work of various classes of workmen :—

			Hours.	Minimum Wage.
Deputies	..	Face-work ..	.. 7½	6/3
„	..	Back-bye shifts	.. ..	5/7
Drivers	..	Under 16 ..	.. 8[1]	2/–
„	..	Over 16 ..	.. 8[1]	2/9
Fillers	..	.. .. ..	.. 8	5/10
Hewers	..	.. .. ..	.. 7	5/6
Onsetters	..	Piece	.. 9½[1]	5/5
„	..	Datal	.. 9½[1]	4/9
Rolleywaymen.		Datal	.. 8[1]	4/9
„	..	Piece.	.. 8[1]	5/2
Shifters	..	.. .. ..	.. 8	4/9
Sinkers	..	.. .. ..	.. 6	5/3
Stonemen.	..	Piece	.. 8	5/5
„	..	Datal	.. 8	4/9
Timber-drawers		Piece	.. 8	5/8
„	..	Datal	.. 8	5/6
Trappers	..	.. .. ..	.. 8[1]	2/–
Wastemen	..	.. .. ..	.. 8	4/9

All other piece-workers receive a minimum wage of 5/– per day, and all other datallers receive a minimum wage of 4/9 per day, according to the award of the Chairman of the Joint District Board. The minimum wage, however, is not paid to hewers over 60 years of age, nor to other workers over 65 years of age.

The minimum wage fixed for youths and lads employed in mines is as follows :—

Datal

Under 15 years	..	..	..	.. 2/– per day.
15 to 16	..	..	..	.. 2/4 „

[1] Hours as ordained by Act of Parliament. Hours of other underground men are bank to bank.

16 to 17	..	..	..	..	.. 2/8 per day.
17 to 18	..	..	..	..	.. 3/– „
18 to 19	..	..	..	..	.. 3/4 „
19 to 20	..	..	..	..	.. 3/8 „
20 to 21	..	..	..	..	.. 4/– „

Piece

Under 19 years	..	..	..	..	4/– per day.
19 to 20		..	..	..	.. 4/3 „
20 to 21	..	..	..	..	.. 4/6 „

As the schedule of hours of adult males shows, the Coal Mines Regulation Act (Eight Hours, 1908), applies to all classes except one, namely, the " onsetters," or men who push the empty " tubs " out of the " cage " at the bottom of the shaft and push the full ones in. These men still work 9½ hours; they are down the mine 10 hours but have half an hour off for meals.

The pits work 11 days a fortnight ; the hewers work 5, 6, 5, 6, 5, 5 shifts in runs of 6 weeks, averaging 5⅓ shifts per week (see p. 159).

All other underground men work one short shift of six hours out of every twelve, thus averaging 47 hours a week.

A study of a miner's pay note shows that he receives certain monetary allowances and payments in kind besides his weekly wages. These are, in the case of certain persons, a free house or 3/– house rent allowance, together with coal to the value of 2/–, (in some cases 1/9). There are, however, certain " off-takes " under the following headings, " Laid Out, Smith Work, Schools, Doctor, Permanent Relief Fund, Water, etc." At certain times hewers have to blast stone and for this purpose they require explosives, which they buy from their employers at the rate of 4½d. per lb. All such expenditure on explosives and powder is placed under the deduction " laid out." Several of these deductions are optional and rest with the employee, but one usually finds that most miners

TABLE V

FULL TIME MONEY WAGES OF ADULT MALES—ALL TRADES

Normal Weekly Wage Rate.	Married House-holders.	Other men over 20 years where known.	All.
Number.	165	82	247
Under 18/–	1	7	8
18/– to 19/–	..	1	1
19/– „ 20/–	..	1	1
20/– „ 21/–	1	1	2
21/– „ 22/–	1	1	2
22/– „ 23/–	..	3	3
23/– „ 24/–	4	1	5
24/– „ 25/–	1	1	2
25/– „ 26/–	3	..	3
26/– „ 27/–	3	2	5
27/– „ 28/–	4	9	13
28/– „ 29/–	7	3	10
29/– „ 30/–	2	5	7
30/– „ 31/–	11	6	17
31/– „ 35/–	39	12	51
35/– „ 40/–	33	14	47
40/– „ 45/–	35	6	41
45/– „ 50/–	10	6	16
50/– „ 55/–	6	1	7
55/– „ 60/–	..	..	..
60/– and over	4	2	6
	Av. about 35/–	Av. about 30/–	Av. about 31/–

contribute to the Permanent Relief Fund, and a good many to the doctor.

In Table V. are stated the wages (exclusive of rent and coal allowance, and of deductions in the case of miners) of 247 adult males employed in mining and other occupations in Stanley. It is found that married householders average a higher wage than do other men over 20 years; the former receive on the average about 35/-, and the latter 30/-. About half the householders earn between 30/- and 40/-, and 16 per cent. between 20/- and 30/-, while there is only one case of a man earning less than £1 a week.

Over 1 in 10 of the male wage-earners over twenty years, other than householders, receive less than £1; but one-fifth receive less than 25/-, while the same proportion receive over £2. Compared with Northampton, for instance, it is found that there is a greater percentage of persons receiving payment at the two extremes. The average is about 30/- in Stanley.

Placing all adult male wage-earners in one group, we find that 4 per cent. earn less than £1, a quarter less than 30/-, over a quarter receive more than £2 a week, while the average wage is about 31/-.

Family Income

The special conditions prevailing in Stanley and arising out of the existence of the coal industry create greater difficulties in the determination of family income than have had to be faced in the other three towns. These complexities are due to the provision of free coal and free houses by the colliery companies.

First let us consider the question of free coal. Those households receive free coal where the head of the family is a miner of a certain grade (see p. 149). The free coal allowance as determined by agreement is 2/- per week, but a large number of cases were found where it was only

1/9. This allowance has been added to the family income. The circumstances of these colliery families will need special consideration, however, when the question of the minimum standard is considered.

TABLE VI

FAMILY INCOME AND RENT

Weekly Rent (including rates and allowing for lodgers)	FAMILY INCOME.						
	Under 10/-	10/- and under 15/-	15/- and under 20/-	20/- and under 25/-	25/- and under 30/-	30/- and under 35/-	35/- and under 40/-
0/- to 9d.	...	...	...	...	...	...	1
1/- „ 1/9	1	...	...	...	...	...	...
2/- „ 2/9	1	...	...	...	2	...	...
3/- „ 3/9	1	...	...	1	1	1	1
4/- „ 4/9	1	...	...	...	...	1	2
5/- „ 5/9	...	...	...	...	4	7	8
6/- „ 6/9	...	...	1	1	...	6	11
7/- „ 7/9	...	...	...	...	...	1	3
8/- „ 8/9	...	...	...	...	1	1	...
9/- „ 9/9	...	...	...	...	...	...	...
10/- „ 10/9	...	...	...	...	...	...	...
11/- „ 11/9	...	...	...	...	...	...	...
Totals	4	...	1	2	8	17	26
Median income	5/6	...	19/-	22/2	27/7	33/6	37/4
Median rent	2/11	...	6/-	4/6	5/-	5/6	6/-
Rent as percentage of income	53	...	32	20	18	16	16

Weekly Rent (including rates and allowing for lodgers)	40/- and under 45/-	45/- and under 50/-	50/- and under 55/-	55/- and under 60/-	60/- and over.	Unknown.	Total.
0/- to 9d.	...	...	...	...	1	...	2
1/- „ 1/9	...	1	...	...	...	...	2
2/- „ 2/9	...	...	...	1	...	...	4
3/- „ 3/9	...	...	...	...	1	1	7
4/- „ 4/9	3	...	...	...	...	...	7
5/- „ 5/9	11	9	3	3	6	2	53
6/- „ 6/9	8	3	2	2	14	1	49
7/- „ 7/9	...	...	2	1	...	...	7
8/- „ 8/9	...	...	...	...	1	...	2
9/- „ 9/9	...	...	...	...	...	...	1
10/- „ 10/9	...	...	...	...	...	...	...
11/- „ 11/9	...	1	...	...	2	...	3
Totals	22	14	7	7	25	4	137
Median income	42/6	48/-	52/9	59/-	80/9	...	...
Median rent	5/6	5/6	6/-	5/6	6/-	...	...
Rent as percentage of income	13	11	11	9	7	...	...

FAMILY INCOME OF PERSONS LIVING IN FREE COLLIERY HOUSES

Under 10/-	10/- and under 15/-	15/- and under 20/-	20/- and under 25/-	25/- and under 30/-	30/- and under 35/-	35/- and under 40/-
...	1	...	2	4	8	11
Median Income.	14/11	...	23/7	29/7½	33/3	36/9

40/- and under 45/-	45/- and under 50/-	50/- and under 55/-	55/- and under 60/-	60/- and over	Unknown	Total
1	7	7	2	22	1	66
41/9	46/-	52/5	57/10	89/3	...	...

Owing to the existence of free houses, the question of lodgers is more difficult than it was in the two preceding chapters. Previously we have regarded each person who receives both board and lodging as contributing one-third of the rent, 2/- as wife's earnings, while the remainder of his payment is assumed to be devoted to his keep. In a colliery house we are unable to take a third off the rent as the dwelling is free ; hence some other means have had to be devised in order to arrive at the amount which the lodger would contribute towards rent if he were in a house for which rent was paid. Though it cannot be said that all colliery houses are worth 6/-, still a family would have to pay about 6/- for a house if they were not residing in a free one. As a lodger usually pays 14/- for board and lodging, it has been assumed in the tabulation of the income of families in Stanley that 10/- is devoted to food, 2/- to wife's earnings and 2/- profit.

In other respects the family income has been computed on the same lines as in the previous chapters.

In Table VI. the family income of those households paying rent is tabulated in relation to the rent paid. It will be seen that over half the income of families with less than 10/- is consumed in rent—this proportion continues to fall nearly regularly as the income increases. The pressure of rent thus falls heaviest on the smaller incomes, gradually decreasing as the income increases, despite the fact that the rent paid by a family increases as the income increases up to about 30/–. Above that amount, income does not appear to be correlated to any extent with rent.

The same table also shows us the distribution of rent-paying households according to their income. The facts can be summarised in the following manner in order to bring out the results more clearly :—

Family Income of less than £1 a week	4	per cent. of number of households.
,, ,, ,, 30/– ,,	11	
,, ,, ,, 40/– ,,	43	
,, ,, ,, 50/– ,,	71	
,, ,, ,, 60/– ,,	81	
,, ,, more ,, 60/– ,,	19	

In other words, of the working-class rent-paying households more than one in ten has a *family* income of less than 30/– a week ; while two households in every five have an income of less than £2 a week, and this in a town where wages are comparatively high.[1]

Family Income in Relation to the Minimum Standard

Official reports relating to Stanley are so few in number that it is only very rarely possible to check our results by comparison with them. As the Board of Trade did not include Stanley in the towns investigated in the Cost of Living enquiry we based our comparisons of

[1] Further, one-quarter of the households have an income of 35/– or less, one-quarter 55/– or more, while half have more than 42/6, and half less than that amount.

The income of those families which live in free colliery houses is given in Table VI. Here again, one-quarter have an income of 35/– or less, but one-third receive more than 60/–, while half have more and half less than 49/–. This shows us a higher level of income among the miners than amongst the rest of the population together with some miners,

food prices upon the data which we collected at the time. It was found upon comparing the prices of commodities most largely consumed by the working-classes, that in the case of food prices were 5 per cent. higher in Stanley than in Northampton and Warrington, while the cost of clothing and sundries was much the same. Coal, we have seen, is given free to some households, and in these cases no expenditure on coal figures in the minimum standard. Best coal would be 15/- per ton to the ordinary householder, but it is only seldom that he buys it at this price; for as the bulk of the population receive more free coal than they consume, the remainder who do not get free coal buy it from those who do at 2/6 per load (14 cwt.). The average household will consume between 4 and 5 cwt. weekly the year round, though in July the average consumption would be about 3 cwt. per week. A simple calculation shows that in the case of those households in which coal has to be bought the minimum weekly expenditure would be about 9d.

Owing to food prices being 5 per cent. higher in Stanley than in other towns, the new food expenditure basis for the former would be as follows :—

FOOD EXPENDITURE BASIS—100 = 4s. 6d.

	Male.	Female.
Over 18 years	105	84
16 to 18 years	89¼	84
14 to 16 years	89¼	73½
5 to 14 years	52½	52½
0 to 5 years	34⅔	34⅔
Old age pensioners and persons over 70	63	52½

Making the necessary allowances for the special circumstances of Stanley, the minimum expenditure of typical families according to the two standards would be as follows :—

	Fuel and State Insurance.	Clothing and Sundries	Food.		Total (including Rent and Fuel).	
			Rowntree Standard	New Standard	Rowntree Standard	New Standard
Man and wife	4d.¹	1/4	7/4	8/6	9/-	10/2
Man, wife and two school children ..	4d.¹	2/6	12/9	13/2	15/7	16/-
Man, wife and three children under 5 years ..	4d.¹	3/1	15/6	13/2	18/11	16/7
Add for each m. ..	..	8d.	3/8	4/8½	..	..
,, ,, f.	..	8d.	3/8	3/9¼	..	..
,, ,, g.	..	7d.	2/8½	3/3¾	..	..
,, ,, l.	..	8d.	3/8	4/-¹	..	..
,, ,, b.	..	7d.	2/8½	4/-¹	..	..
,, ,, sc.	..	7d.	2/8½	2/4½	..	..
,, ,, in.	..	7d.	2/8½	1/6¾	..	..

Placing the income of families in relation to these two standards, it is found that 11 families fall below both and that one other falls below the York Standard. These 12 households contain 6 per cent. of the working-class population investigated, so that we may state that from 4 to 8 per cent. (see p. 181) of the working-class population of Stanley are below the standard necessary for the maintenance of physical health. This result compares very favourably with Northampton and the other towns. But nevertheless poverty does exist, though, as in 5 out of the 12 cases poor relief is known to be given, it would be wrong to say that 6 per cent. of the working-class population are in distress. It is probable that in some of the other cases assistance is received from relatives, friends and charities ; on the other hand, it has been assumed that every wage-earner is in permanent employment.

¹ If coal is not obtained free, then 9d. must be added.

In Table VII. the 203 households are shown in their position above and below the standards :—

TABLE VII

FAMILIES ABOVE AND BELOW THE POVERTY LINE

RELATION TO MR. ROWNTREE'S STANDARD.				RELATION TO NEW STANDARD.			
Above.	No. of Households.	Below.	No. of Households.	Above.	No. of Households.	Below.	No. of Households.
Shillings.		Shillings.		Shillings.		Shillings.	
40 and over	40	−14 ,, 15	1	+ 40 & over	40	−13 ,, 14	1
+35 to 40	13	−13 ,, 14	1	+35 to 40	10	−12 ,, 13	..
+30 ,, 35	10	−12 ,, 13	..	+30 ,, 35	12	−11 ,, 12	..
+25 ,, 30	15	−11 ,, 12	..	+25 ,, 30	16	−10 ,, 11	1
+20 ,, 25	29	−10 ,, 11	..	+20 ,, 25	24	− 9 ,, 10	..
+18 ,, 20	13	− 9 ,, 10	..	+18 ,, 20	17	− 8 ,, 9	1
+16 ,, 18	9	− 8 ,, 9	2	+16 ,, 18	14	− 7 ,, 8	1
+14 ,, 16	14	− 7 ,, 8	..	+14 ,, 16	10	− 6 ,, 7	1
+12 ,, 14	11	− 6 ,, 7	1	+12 ,, 14	17	− 5 ,, 6	..
+10 ,, 12	12	− 5 ,, 6	..	+10 ,, 12	6	− 4 ,, 5	..
+ 8 ,, 10	8	− 4 ,, 5	..	+ 8 ,, 10	9	− 3 ,, 4	
+ 7 ,, 8	1	− 3 ,, 4	1	+ 7 ,, 8	4	− 2 ,, 3	1
+ 6 ,, 7	3	− 2 ,, 3	2	+ 6 ,, 7	2	− 1 ,, 2	2
+ 5 ,, 6	2	− 1 ,, 2	1	+ 5 ,, 6	..	− 0 ,, 1	..
+ 4 ,, 5	3	− 0 ,, 1	1	+ 4 ,, 5	5	Unknown	1
+ 3 ,, 4	4	Unknown	2	+ 3 ,, 4	..		2
+ 2 ,, 3	..			+ 2 ,, 3	1		
+ 1 ,, 2	..			+ 1 ,, 2	1		
+ 0 ,, 1	1			+ 0 ,, 1	1		
	188		12		189		11

Remaining houses ; —At line, 2. Omitted, 1.

If an analysis of the causes of the deficiency of income is made (see p. 40), it is found that in

3 cases, the immediate cause was " Death of the chief wage-earner."

6 cases, the immediate cause was " Illness or old age of chief wage-earner."

1 case, the immediate cause was " Largeness of family."

2 cases, the immediate cause was that wages were below the standard for 3 children.

	EARNING.					
	Men over 20.	Women over 16.	Girls 14–16.	Sons 18–20.	Lads & Boys 14–18.	Total.
Below New Standard ..	4	4	1	1	2	12
Total	279	15	1	17	17	329
Percentage below ..	1	27	100	6	12	4

	DEPENDENT.					
	Men over 18.	Women.	Girls, Lads & Boys.	School Children.	Infants.	Total.
Below New Standard ..	6	9	0	25	8	48
Total	22	242	26	214	142	646
Percentage below ..	27	4	0	12	6	7

	EARNING AND DEPENDENT.				
	Men.	Women	Girls, Lads, and Boys over 14.	Children and Infants under 14.	Total.
Percentage below	3	5	6½	9	6

Persons below, 60 ; persons above, 715 ; total, 775.

The Table above gives a classification of households according to the number of dependent children and to the relation to the minimum standard. The tabulation is, however, of less value than the similar Tables made in the previous chapters, where, owing to the larger number of observations, more definite conclusions could be made. Of the 172 households headed by an adult male wage earner, 3 (2 per cent.) are below both standards, while of the 19 cases where the father is ill, dead or absent, one-quarter are below.

An analysis of the constitution of families below the poverty line is of interest as showing the percentage of school children who live in them.

Though the percentage of school children falling below the standard is much smaller than in the other towns, it is, nevertheless, considerable. To realise that one school child in every eight is in this unfortunate position in a centre where wages are high compared with the general level of wages in other towns must deepen the impression made by the appalling conditions already shown to exist in Reading and Warrington.

NOTE.—(*Budgets*). Great difficulty was experienced in obtaining persons who would keep household budgets of the nature required, and finally the task had to be abandoned. One or two budgets were kept for a week, but these are not published as they might be misleading.

NOTE.—(*Days and Shifts*). The pits at Stanley are at work 11 days per fortnight, ceasing on alternate Saturdays. On Saturdays, when the pit is working, only two short shifts are worked, on other days three shifts. The men change week by week from the first to the mid-shift, and from the mid-shift on the last. When on the last shift they have no work on Saturday. Thus each man works on two Saturdays only in six weeks.

CHAPTER V

READING

(*Summarised from the Journal of the Royal Statistical Society*, 1912-13, pp. 672-701[1])

THE investigation made in Reading in the autumn of 1912 was the first in time of this series, and its success in providing new and important information led to the further enquiries already described. The experience gained in Reading was of great use in facilitating the later work, both in saving time and expense, and in showing the points as to which the answers needed special checking ; it is probable that in the later enquiries greater accuracy was obtained.

Reading industrially resembles York rather than the other towns dealt with, in that it is a town with considerable county business, is an important railway centre, contains a certain number of engineering and printing firms, but has no industry on a large scale except the manufacture of food, which employs a specially large proportion of unskilled workers. In Reading, however, the principal biscuit company, though it does not, as is sometimes supposed, exhaust the town's activities, is relatively very large, and probably employs directly a quarter or a fifth of the working class. The result is that in Reading there is an unusually large proportion of unskilled workers, whose wages are low and probably prevented from rising by the low scale of agricultural wages in Berkshire and Oxfordshire.

---

[1] Some minor corrections have been made.

The population Census shows (for the present borough) in April, 1911 :—

	Number.	Population.
Inhabited dwelling-houses and flats..	17,302	78,291
Empty..	1,559	..
Inhabited shops	1,194	5,377
Hotels, &c., offices, workshops, &c., and miscellaneous	356	1,644
Institutions	92	2,381
Uninhabited buildings	822	..
	21,325	87,693

At the date of the investigation there were probably about 18,000 inhabited dwelling-houses, of which 840 (working-class or superior) came under review, that is 1 in 21½. The *multiplier twenty-one and one-half* is then to be applied to all the sample data to give estimates for the whole of Reading.

The tables are framed in precisely the same way as those of the corresponding headings in the previous chapters.

It appears that 63 per cent. of the houses are five-roomed, and that half of these are rented at from 6/– to 6/9 ; while 20 per cent. are four-roomed houses, of which more than half are rented at from 5/– to 5/9. (Table I., next page.)

Table II. shows the number of persons in relation to the number of rooms. In 9 cases the Census definition of overcrowding (more than 2 persons to a room) is reached ; in 12 cases (shown in heavy type) there are exactly 2 persons ; in 154, between 1 and 2 persons ; and in 434, 1 person or less. In 1911, Reading was among the best

L

TABLE I

NUMBER OF ROOMS OF WORKING-CLASS HOUSES, CLASSIFIED ACCORDING TO RENTS AND ROOMS

Weekly Rent (including Rates).	Number of Rooms.								Totals.
	1.	2.	3.	4.	5.	6.	7.	8.	
2/– to 2/9 ..	1	1	2	..	..	..	..	..	4
3/– ,, 3/9 ..	..	1	13	3	..	..	..	..	17
4/– ,, 4/9 ..	..	..	2	21	3	1	..	..	27
5/– ,, 5/9 ..	..	..	..	70	83	1	..	..	154
6/– ,, 6/9 ..	..	..	3	28	188	14	..	..	233
7/– ,, 7/9 ..	..	..	..	2	80	23	3	..	108
8/– ,, 8/9 ..	..	..	..	..	18	11	4	1	34
9/– ,, 9/9 ..	..	..	..	..	5	2	4	1	12
10/– ,, 10/9 ..	..	..	..	..	1	4	4	1	10
11/– ,, 11/9 ..	..	..	..	..	..	3	1	1	5
12/– ..	..	..	..	..	..	1	..	..	1
Totals ..	1	2	20	124	378	60	16	4	605
Median rents ..	..	2/6	3/7	5/6	6/6	7/7	9/1	9/9	6/3
Median rent per room ..	..	1/3	1/2	1/4½	1/3½	1/3	1/3½	1/0½	1/3

TABLE II

NUMBER OF WORKING-CLASS HOUSES CLASSIFIED ACCORDING TO THE NUMBER OF PERSONS AND OF ROOMS

Number of Rooms.	Number of Persons.												Totals.
	1.	2.	3.	4.	5.	6.	7.	8.	9.	10.	11.	12.	
1	..	1	..	..	..	..	..	..	..	..	..	..	1
2	3	1	..	0	..	..	..	..	..	..	..	..	4
3	4	5	5	1	2	0	2	..	..	1	..	..	20
4	5	25	25	19	18	13	9	5	4	1	..	..	124
5	4	42	83	82	61	50	25	19	7	6	..	1	380
6	..	11	14	10	10	6	4	1	3	..	1	0	60
7	..	1	6	1	2	1	4	..	..	1	..	..	16
8	..	..	..	..	1	2	..	1	..	..	..	..	4
Tls.	16	86	133	113	94	72	44	26	14	9	1	1	609

of the County Boroughs when judged by this test of overcrowding.

When we take the new standard of crowding we find that there are 84 cases of overcrowding, 27 cases on the line, and 498 cases above.

TABLE III

NUMBER OF WORKING-CLASS HOUSES CLASSIFIED ACCORD-
ING TO THE NUMBER OF EQUIVALENT ADULTS AND OF
ROOMS

Number of Rooms.	1	1¼	1½	2	2¼	2½	2¾	3	3¼	3½	3¾	4	4¼	4½	4¾
1	0	..	..	1	..	..	..	..	..	..	..	..	..	..	..
2	3	..	..	1	..	..	..	..	..	..	..	..	..	..	..
3	4	..	..	5	1	..	1	3	..	1	1	1	1	..	2
4	5	1	..	24	8	13	9	10	11	2	6	8	10	2	3
5	4	..	1	43	22	31	28	45	23	20	21	34	14	20	13
6	..	2	..	9	..	6	..	12	6	2	1	4	5	1	4
7	..	..	..	1	1	1	1	3	1	..	..	1	..	1	1
8	..	..	..	..	..	..	..	..	..	..	..	..	..	1	..
Totals	16	3	1	84	32	51	39	73	41	25	29	48	30	25	23

Number of Rooms.	5	5¼	5½	5¾	6	6¼	6½	6¾	7	7¼	7½	7¾	8	Totals.
1	..	..	..	..	..	..	..	..	..	..	..	..	..	1
2	..	..	..	..	..	..	..	..	..	..	..	..	..	4
3	..	..	..	..	..	..	..	..	..	..	..	..	..	20
4	7	1	1	..	1	2	..	..	..	..	..	..	..	124
5	13	11	7	10	6	2	4	4	..	1	1	2	..	380
6	3	..	..	2	1	..	..	..	..	..	1	..	1	60
7	..	1	..	1	1	1	..	..	1	..	..	..	..	16
8	2	..	..	..	1	..	..	..	..	..	..	..	0	4
Totals	25	13	8	13	10	5	4	4	1	1	2	2	1	609

Classification of the households is difficult, for, allowing for the 10 sub-divisions and the distinction between earner and non-earner, there are about 260 different groupings in 609 households. The statistician's normal family of man (at work), wife (not working) and 3 dependent children only occurs 33 times.

Table IV. shows the main lines of division. The arrangement differs in the fourth and fifth divisions from that used p. 220, Table IV.[2].

TABLE IV

EARNERS AND DEPENDENT CHILDREN

Man alone earning.		Man and one or more children earning.		Man and wife earning.[1]	
Dependent children of all ages.	Number of households.	Dependent children of all ages.	Number of households.	Dependent children of all ages.	Number of households.
0	65	0	62	0	11
1	69	1	26	1	6
2	58	2	24	2	9
3	36	3	26	3	7
4	23	4	13	4	3
5	12	5	7	..	..
6	9	6	4	..	..
7	6	..	..	..	..
8	1	..	..	..	..
Not known	11	..	..	..	..
	290[1]		162[1]		36

[1] In all cases but 21 the wife is living. There are also 32 adult non-earners in the first group and 21 in the second.

[2] In 16 cases one or more children are also earning.

Other cases where at least one man over 20 years is working.		Women, girls and lads under 20 earning.[1]		No earnings.	
Dependent children of all ages.	Number of households.	Dependent children of all ages.	Number of households.	Dependent children of all ages.	Number of households.
0	27	0	32	0	28
1	10	1	7	1	3
2	9	2	3	2	1
3	3	3	2	4	3
4	1	4	2	..	..
5	1	5	1	..	..
7	1	..	..	..	..
	52		47		35

Rates of Wages

The following rates of wages are, as explained elsewhere, derived from statements made by the wage-earners or their wives, criticised and adjusted in the light of general information, but not checked by reference to the employers.

The higher average for householders whose wages were estimated is due to the fact that, the better off people were, the less willing did they prove to give information.

It appears that the average wage for a full week's work for men over 20 years of age in Reading is about 24/6. A similar average for York, in 1899, was 26/6.[2] Since then wages in general have risen about 10 per cent., but Reading remains 2/– below where York was. The

[1] One woman only in 26 cases, including 3 with 1 child, 1 with 3, and 1 with 5 children.
[2] *Journal of the Royal Statistical Society*, 1902, p. 359. Men over 18; if over 20 had been taken, it might be nearer 271.

TABLE V

FULL-TIME WAGES OF ADULT MALES. ALL TRADES

Normal weekly wage rate.	Married householders.			Other men over 20 years where known (including lodgers).	Total.
	Stated.	Estimated.	Together.		
Number ..	296	178	474	54	528
Under 18/–	6	8	14	23	37
18/– to 19/–	16	12	28	5	33
19/– ,, 20/–	8	3	11	1	12
20/– ,, 21/–	51	17	68	7	75
21/– ,, 22/–	39	14	53	3	56
22/– ,, 23/–	24	9	33	1	34
23/– ,, 24/–	14	5	19	2	21
24/– ,, 25/–	22	10	32	3	35
25/– ,, 26/–	28	25	53	2	55
26/– ,, 27/–	5	1	6	3	9
27/– ,, 28/–	12	5	17	1	18
28/– ,, 29/–	6	1	7	..	7
29/– ,, 30/–	6	0	6	..	6
30/– ,, 31/–	23	34	57	1	58
31/– ,, 35/–	15	5	20	1	21
35/– ,, 40/–	14	15	29	1	30
40/– and over	7	14	21	..	21
Approx. Average..	24/6	26/–	25/–	20/–	24/6

general average for men in industrial occupations in 1906 in the United Kingdom was about 29/–,[1] and by 1913 must have been 30/–. It thus appears that the average in Read-

[1] Wage Census of 1906 *passim.*

ing is relatively very low. This is, of course, connected with the absence of any industries employing a large proportion of skilled men, and with the close connection between Reading and the surrounding agricultural districts.

Note as to Wages of Lads and Girls

From our cards it appears that a girl of 14 or 15 would get about 5/6 at a factory or printing works, whereas if she went into daily service she would get 2/– to 3/– and food. If she was apprenticed to a dressmaker she would probably get 1/– or 2/–. At the age of 17 she would be getting about 7/– at a factory, and about 4/6 with a dressmaker, 7/– with a tailor, and about 5/6 at a laundry. She would probably be earning 8/6 at a factory when she was 19, and later about 11/–.

A boy of 14 or 15 would get about 6/6 at a factory or workshop, and about 5/– as an office boy, clerk or errand boy. At 17 and 18, in a factory, he would be getting 8/– or 9/–, whereas as a shop assistant it would be rather less than 9/–. At 18 and 19, at a factory and in most trades, he would get about 10/– or 11/–, though as a clerk he would be earning 12/– or 13/–, or more. At the age of 22 he would probably be getting £1 a week in unskilled work.

Family Income and Rent

Table VI. shows the relation between rent paid and family income calculated on the basis discussed elsewhere. The incomes below 15/– are probably supplemented by charity or poor relief. The proportion spent on rent falls regularly as the income increases, and may appear low to those who are used to computing rent in relation to one adult workman's wages. It is probable that if married clerks and others with an income of £150 to £200 were included, we should find rent (including rates and water) formed a higher proportion than in the case of the higher

working-class family incomes.   In fact, however, a study
of the insufficient incomes dealt with below shows that
in Reading other expenditures give way and food is allowed
to fall below Mr. Rowntree's standard, while a fairly good
house in a respectable street (sometimes with more than
the minimum accommodation) is rented.   The desire
for an adequate garden is so great that many workmen
live outside the town (but generally within the recently
extended borough) to secure one.

Family Income and the Minimum Standard

Taking the Rowntree standard as explained above
(p. 82) we find 128 households almost certainly below the
standard, and 17 others probably below, out of 622.
These 145 households contain 29 per cent. of the working-
class population in our sample, and we may affirm that,
on the basis described, from 25 to 30 per cent. of the
working-class population of Reading were in 1912, so
far as they were dependent on their earnings, pensions
or possessions, below Mr. Rowntree's standard, whereas
in York, in 1899, only 15½ per cent. of the working-class
population was below this standard.   Of the *whole* population 19 per cent. is below the line ; Mr. Rowntree found
10 per cent.

This is not the same thing as saying that 25 to 30 per
cent. of the working-class are near destitution, or even
in poverty.   In eight of the 145 cases poor-relief is known
to be given, and it is probable in five others ; in some cases
it is known that absent relatives assist.   There is a large
number of charities and many charitable persons in Reading, and it is likely that clothes are often obtained.   But
it is not probable that gifts, doles and subsidies lift any
large proportion of these families over the line ; in general
they only remove the destitution but leave a deficiency.
In a register of the families who have obtained or applied
for assistance from public or private sources in the

TABLE VI—Family Income and Rent

Weekly Rents (including Rates and Allowing for Lodgers).	FAMILY INCOME.												Totals
	Under 10/-	10/- and under 15/-	15/- and under 20/-	20/- and under 25/-	25/- and under 30/-	30/- and under 35/-	35/- and under 40/-	40/- and under 45/-	45/- and under 50/-	50/- and under 55/-	55/- and under 60/-	60/- and over.	
2/- to 2/9	2	3	·	1	·	·	·	·	·	·	·	·	6
3/- „ 3/9	5	7	3	4	3	2	1	1	·	·	·	·	26
4/- „ 4/9	3	4	4	15	10	5	5	1	1	2	1	1	52
5/- „ 5/9	2	3	17	52	24	23	16	9	5	1	·	2	154
6/- „ 6/9	3	6	9	45	42	41	20	19	9	7	5	9	215
7/- „ 7/9	·	·	2	13	13	17	17	10	10	4	2	7	95
8/- „ 8/9	·	·	·	1	2	3	6	·	3	1	2	3	21
9/- „ 9/9	·	·	·	·	·	·	1	2	·	1	1	1	6
10/- „ 10/9	·	·	·	·	·	·	1	3	·	2	·	1	7
11/- „ 11/9	·	·	·	·	·	·	·	2	·	·	·	2	4
Totals ..	15	23	35	131	94	91	67	47	28	18	11	26	586
Median income	6/9	10/9	18/6	21/9	26/9	31/3	36/9	41/9	47/-	52/6	57/-	67/-	29/6
Median rent ..	4/-	4/-	5/6	5/9	6/-	6/-	6/6	6/6	6/6	6/9	6/9	7/-	6/-
Rent as per cent. of income	59	37	30	25	22	19	17½	16	14	13	12	10½	20

twenty-six months beginning March, 1911, are 4,623 entries. In our sample we might expect about 220 of these.

The table below shows the constitution of the households below, or probably below, the Standards. Out of 520 households headed by an adult male wage-earner, 111 (21 per cent.) are below one or both standards. Of 145 households where a sole male wage-earner has 2 or more children dependent, 81 (56 per cent.) are below. As the number of wage-earners increases, even if it is only a young lad or girl earning as well as the father, more younger children can be supported. Of 67 households where the father is ill, absent or deceased, 23 are below.

Of the 95 working-class lodgers, it is estimated that 24 (4 m, 12 f, 5 sc, and 3 in) live below the new standard. Including these, but omitting 4 households as to whose constitution information is wanting, we obtain the following table :—

	EARNING.					
	Men over 20.	Women over 16.	Girls under 16.	Sons 18–20.	Lads and Boys 14 to 18.	Total.
Below New standard	110	43	9	3	23	188
Total	677	225	34	41	97	1,075
Percentage below	16	19	26	7	24	17½

	DEPENDENT.					
	Men over 18.	Women.	Girls.	Lads & Boys.	School Children.	Infants.	Total.
Below standard	16	135	1	4	286	152	594
Total	50	573	9	11	623	334	1,600
Percentage below.	32	23½	11	36	45½	45	37

	EARNING AND DEPENDENT.				All.
	Men.	Women.	Girls, lads and boys over 14.	Children and infants under 14.	
Percentage below	17½	22	20	46	29

Persons below, 782; persons above, 1,893; total, 2,675.

Table VII. shows by how much the households fell short. One hundred and eleven of the 144 failed by more than 2/–, and 66 by more than 5/–. Perhaps the 2/– might be made up in good times; but it is not possible to reduce the total number actually short of adequate food and clothing much on any hypothesis, for we have assumed that all earnings are economically spent and that employment is perfect. Actually, 19[1] households more would have been counted below the line if we had taken the amount of employment in the week previous to the visit in each case as typical, insteading of assuming full employment, and the autumn of 1912 was a specially busy time.

About 45 per cent. of the children under 5 years in working-class houses, and 47 per cent. of the school children in the public elementary schools[2] appear to have been living in households below the standard at the time of the enquiry. The actual proportion of children who at some period before they are 14 years old are in such households must be much higher than this; for of the other children enumerated in Table II[R]. App. some have recently passed above the line owing to their elder sisters

[1] In 6 other households the distance below the line would have been increased, and 15 more would have a smaller excess, if the earnings of the particular week had been taken.

[2] In 1912, 1,407 children from 512 houses were given free meals at one time or another by the Education Committee. This number is larger than usual, owing to an excess during the coal strike. In January, 1912, the number was 851, besides 71 in Whitley Special School.

TABLE VII

FAMILIES ABOVE AND BELOW THE POVERTY LINE INCLUDING THOSE "PROBABLY" BELOW

RELATION TO MR. ROWNTREE'S STANDARD.				RELATION TO NEW STANDARD.			
Above.	No. of house-holds.	Below.	No. of house-holds.	Above.	No. of house-holds.	Below.	No. of house-holds.
+ 40/-	7	—22/-	2	+ 40/-	4	—24/-	1
+ 35 to 40	11	—21 to 22	1	+ 35 to 40	11	—20 to 24	1
+ 30 ,, 35	6	—20 ,, 21	1	+ 30 ,, 35	6	—18 ,, 19	2
+ 25 ,, 30	17	—19 ,, 20	1	+ 25 ,, 30	13	—17 ,, 18	1
+ 20 ,, 25	30	—18 ,, 19	1	+ 20 ,, 25	26	—16 ,, 17	3
+ 18 ,, 20	17	—17 ,, 18	2	+ 18 ,, 20	16	—15 ,, 16	2
+ 16 ,, 18	13	—16 ,, 17	2	+ 16 ,, 18	20	—14 ,, 15	1
+ 14 ,, 16	31	—15 ,, 16	1	+ 14 ,, 16	17	—12 ,, 13	2
+ 12 ,, 14	31	—14 ,, 15	3	+ 12 ,, 14	37	—11 ,, 12	4
+ 10 ,, 12	37	—13 ,, 14	1	+ 10 ,, 12	33	—10 ,, 11	10
+ 8 ,, 10	42	—12 ,, 13	3	+ 8 ,, 10	42	— 9 ,, 10	4
+ 7 ,, 8	20	—11 ,, 12	4	+ 7 ,, 8	23	— 8 ,, 9	6
+ 6 ,, 7	28	—10 ,, 11	6	+ 6 ,, 7	29	— 7 ,, 8	10
+ 5 ,, 6	26	— 9 ,, 10	8	+ 5 ,, 6	27	— 6 ,, 7	6
+ 4 ,, 5	22	— 8 ,, 9	8	+ 4 ,, 5	19	— 5 ,, 6	13
+ 3 ,, 4	18	— 7 ,, 8	7	+ 3 ,, 4	24	— 4 ,, 5	16
+ 2 ,, 3	27	— 6 ,, 7	5	+ 2 ,, 3	31	— 3 ,, 4	16
+ 1 ,, 2	21	— 5 ,, 6	13	+ 1 ,, 2	28	— 2 ,, 3	13
+ 0 ,, 1	48	— 4 ,, 5	23	+ 0 ,, 1	50	— 1 ,, 2	22
Amount not known	25	— 3 ,, 4	15	Amount not known	22	— 0 ,, 1	6
		— 2 ,, 3	13			Amount not known	5
		— 1 ,, 2	16				
		— 0 ,, 1	4				
		Amount not known	5				
	477		145		478		144

Those "possibly below" are included in "amount not known" above.

or brothers getting to work, and some will fall below the line owing to the arrival of competitors for food as yet unborn. The wage statistics given in table V., read in conjunction with the standard table, support the view that more than half the working-class children of Reading, during some part of their first fourteen years, live in households where the standard of life in question is not attained.

TABLE VIII

HOUSEHOLDS BELOW THE POVERTY LINE

Immediate cause.	Percentage of households below the standard.	
	York.	Reading.
Death of chief wage-earner ..	27	14
Illness or old age of chief wage-earner	10	11
Chief wage-earner out of work	3	2
Irregularity of work	3	4
Largeness of family, *i.e.*, more than four children	13	20
In regular work, but at low wages	44	49
	100	100

The immediate causes of deficiency of income in Reading can be compared with Mr. Rowntree's table for York.[1] A slightly different classification was given on p. 40 above.

In York the first two classes, where there is no man earning, account for 3·3 per cent. of the households of the city ; in Reading, about 4 per cent. The main reason for the greater poverty of Reading is therefore due to relative lowness of wages ; or, to put the same thing in other words, the wages of unskilled labour are not sufficient in Reading, and were not in York, to support a family of three or more children.

[1] *Poverty*, edition 1908, p. 120.

NOTE.—The table showing in detail the numbers of families of various composition can be consulted in the *Statistical Journal* 1912-3, pp. 697 *seq.*, where also five budgets of expenditure are given.

CHAPTER VI

CRITICISM OF THE ACCURACY OF THE RESULTS

THERE are four possible sources of uncertainty or error in an investigation as to social conditions such as forms the subject of this book. The information obtained may be incorrect; the definitions and standards used may be loose, unsuitable, or wrongly conceived; the households actually visited may not contain a fair sample of the whole population; and there are also calculable possibilities of error arising from the process of estimating the whole by measuring a part.

I.—There is no reasonable doubt as to the conscientiousness and capability of the majority of the investigators, and there were many ways in which the *prima facie* reasonableness of the information written on the cards could be checked, since those in local charge were, or made themselves, well acquainted with the general conditions of the towns and the ordinary rates of wages. Where there was evident improbability, and where there was incompleteness, further information was obtained, if possible, and in doubtful cases (especially when near the poverty line) the households were placed in the categories of " possible " or " probable " in Tables IV., App. In Northampton and Warrington wage statements were checked in a considerable number of cases by definite facts from the employers, and the result was to show that there was no evident bias in the direction of overstatement or understatement, though there were mistakes and misunderstandings as to the meaning of the phrase " full time earnings " on both sides, inherent in the general vagueness of the conception of a week's earnings. It is believed that uncertainty from this cause, in the case of persons in ordinary work, has not affected perceptibly the proportions found. In the case of earnings of ill-defined, irregular or casual occupations, there is more uncertainty, and such cases account for the entries in the columns " possibly " and " probably below standard." The division between " possibly " and " probably " was made by a review of all the known circumstances of the household. It is believed that these categories contain all the doubtful cases.

No very serious attempt was made to find all income other than earnings. Actual property, especially house property, was most likely generally known, but this seldom concerns persons not fairly well off ; pensions from employers and old-age pensions, which were added to household earnings, were not difficult to hear of.[1] In many cases we heard of poor relief, relatives' regular or intermittent assistance, and in some of organised or private charity ; but as these were excluded from our definition of income, and also were rarely sufficient to raise the family above poverty, we did not search assiduously for this kind of income, and no doubt did not learn all the resources of all the families.

The number of cases in which information was refused at a house, and could not be obtained elsewhere, was relatively small ; but there were more cases where the amount of the man's actual wages was not given, and had to be deduced from his occupation.

So far as household earnings, as defined for our purpose, were concerned, we may conclude that we had sufficient means for forming a judgment in the great majority of

[1] In Reading we found too few Old-Age Pensioners, even allowing for their possible residence in institutions. Where persons appeared to be over 70, and the household only needed a pension to bring it above the line, it was treated as uncertain.

cases, and that the margin of uncertainty is sufficiently allowed for by the margin given in the Tables and reports.

On subjects other than earnings, *viz.* :—occupations, relationship, dependence, kind of house, etc., there is every reason to believe that our data are nearly accurate. The tests given below show in particular that the numbers of school children especially were well ascertained, and that the occupations were correctly stated. Houses so generally belong to one of a small number of well-known types, that there was no difficulty in placing them. Generally the information given in Tables I. to IV. in each chapter and I. and II. in Appendix may be depended upon.

II.—The definition of " the working class " cannot be exactly drawn on preconceived lines. Of course, in the great majority of cases included in our Tables the principal occupant of the house was working for weekly or hourly wages, and in the great majority of houses in our samples treated as non-working class the occupier was professional, commercial or living on income from property. The necessity for less obvious discrimination arose in houses rented at from 7/6 to 12/– a week. If the principal occupants were clerks, travellers, teachers, shop managers or employers in a small way they were excluded from the working-class Tables. Shop assistants were only included in the working-class if working for butchers or grocers. The great majority of shop assistants are, of course, not householders, but living with their parents. The working-class householders include among their supplementary earners a not very large number of persons, who would, if principal occupants, have been excluded.[1] A small number of the working-class, other than domestic servants, are (at any rate in Reading) caretakers or nominal occupiers of better class houses in which the married

[1] For an analysis of the mixture of classes see " The Measurement of Social Phenomena " (P. S. King & Son), where some tables based on the statistics of this enquiry are given.

woman acts as domestic servant while the husband works in the town. The whole number in these doubtful margins is, however, very small.

The definition of lodger presented some difficulties. In general, relatives of the principal occupier were not counted as lodgers, whatever money arrangements were made, and others who paid were counted as lodgers. In making up the family income very careful allowance was made for lodgers' payments.

The most contentious definition is that of the minimum standard. We have kept as closely as possible to Mr. Rowntree's standard, and its meaning and justification are fully dealt with in his *Poverty*. The alterations made for change of prices, amount of fuel, cost of light, and compulsory insurance are so small that the margin of uncertainty attaching to them is negligible.

The alternative standard may be regarded as arbitrary, but reasonable. It does not profess to measure a minimum necessary for efficiency ; but it is a measure adaptable to families of different compositions, and to different places and circumstances. Any one familiar with working-class life can picture the standard that is reached with expenditure on food at the prices of 1913 of 4/6 a week for a man, 3/8 for a woman and an average of 2/3 for school children and of 1/6 for those under 5 years. Though it cannot be said in specific terms that a family which does not reach this standard is poor, while one that does reach it is not poor, yet it makes an intelligible line by which we can divide the population, and by the use of which we can compare towns. It is probable, also, that a family with an income which allows for this expenditure just about reaches Mr. Rowntree's standard of nutriment if it is judiciously spent on economic lines. There is then no ambiguity in the statement that a certain family, if it depended on its earnings and property, would be below this standard.

M

The definition of a room is sometimes difficult, so that overcrowding measurements have a margin of uncertainty (see Warrington), and must be interpreted in the light of the descriptions of housing given in chapters II.–V. and the appendix.

III.—There is very little doubt that the households were so chosen as to make a fair and unbiassed sample of that part of the population that lives in private houses. For each town a list of all houses, as given in a directory for Reading and Northampton, and in the assessment lists and burgess rolls elsewhere, was obtained, and without reference to anything except the accidental order (alphabetical by streets or otherwise) in the list, one entry in twenty was ticked. The buildings so marked, other than shops, institutions, factories, etc., formed the sample. Very strict instructions were given that no house which was occupied should be omitted, however difficult it was to get information, and the number of cases where other houses were substituted is practically negligible. The few cases where no basis for estimating income could be obtained were quite as frequent among the relatively well off as among the destitute. The sample is equally fair as regards the rich and the poor ; but in fact we did not attempt to investigate upper-class houses, except in Reading, where we ascertained their assessed values. It is possible that some of the worst tenements are not named in the directories, but we found no evidence that this was the case. Some uncertainty comes from the omission from the working-class of resident domestic servants, shop-assistants sleeping at the shop, small shop-keepers and caretakers. These are in practically all cases above the standard. Their inclusion would result in the percentage of *persons* in the working-class below the standard being lowered slightly ; the percentage of households is, of course, unaffected.

IV.—The adequacy of a fair sample of one in twenty

must now be considered. It is evident that averages based on one house in twenty in every street in a town must give a composite result that is closely related to a result based on complete information, and that there is no reason why any percentage or average obtained should be in excess rather than in defect. It is further evident that the larger the number taken in the sample the more accurate will be the picture, and that the more general features will be presented with less uncertainty than the less common. It is also well known that there is a peculiar safety in the process of averaging, that the whole principle of insurance rests on this principle, and that a great variety of commercial transactions depends on measurement by sampling. Again, scientific men are generally aware that the security of averaging can be tested by mathematical analysis. On the other hand, a sample of 1 in 20 only will appear to afford too slender a basis, and very few persons other than mathematicians are acquainted with the methods by which accuracy is foretold, or with the numerical precision that comes from any given proportion or number of samples.

It happens that the particular process of selection used leads to results whose accuracy can be described in a simple form. Suppose that, in a group of N things, there are $p \times N$ which have some assigned character, and that n out of N things are chosen at random and examined, then it is more likely that the exact proportion $p \times n$ in the selected group will be found to have the character than any other individual number, and small deviations from this number are more probable than large. Thus, if 800 houses are examined in a town containing 16,000 houses, and 10 per cent. in the town are four-roomed, then 10 per cent. of 800, $i.e.$, 80, is the most probable number of four-roomed houses that will be found in the sample (though such exactness will not often be reached), and it is more likely that 75 or 85 will be found than 70 or

90. There is, in fact, a general table of probability applicable to such a case. It is proved that it is just as likely as not—the odds are equal—that the number found in the sample will differ from pn by as much as $\frac{2}{3}$ of $\sqrt{p\,(1-p)\,n}$. This quantity is called the *probable error* of the measurement. Conversely, it can be shown that (unless p is very small) if $p'n$ examples are found in n trials, it is as likely as not that the proportion in the whole group will differ from p' by as much as $\frac{2}{3}\sqrt{\dfrac{(p'\,(1-p').}{n}}$ When the " probable error " is established, the tables of probability show that the fact will differ from the forecast by three times this error only once in 25 experiments in the long run, and by four or five times this error so seldom that the chance of so great a deviation is negligible.

On this basis we can make a table showing the probable error in the case of 800 houses, which will give a guide to the Reading, Northampton and Warrington investigations, and for 200 houses for West Stanley. The first column shows varying percentages of houses in the sample that have some assigned characteristic (p' of the last paragraph expressed as a percentage).

Percentage found in Sample. 100 p'				Probable error. $n=800$	$n=200$
5 per cent.	..	..	..	·5	1
10 ,,	..	..	..	·7	1·4
15 ,,	..	..	..	·84	1·7
20 ,,	..	..	..	·94	1·9
25 ,,	..	..	..	1·0	2·0
30 ,,	..	..	..	1·08	2·2
35 ,,	..	..	..	1·12	2·2
40 ,,	..	..	..	1·15	2·3
45 ,,	..	..	..	1·17	2·3
50 ,,	..	..	..	1·2	2·4

Thus, for example, if in Reading 20 per cent. of the houses in the sample are found to be four-roomed, we deduce that the number of four-roomed working-class houses in the borough is as likely as not to differ from 20 per cent. of all working-class houses by ·94 per cent., *i.e.*, as likely as not to be between 19·06 and 20·94, and is very unlikely to differ by $(3 \times ·94 =)$ 2·8, and practically certain not to differ by $(5 \times ·94 =)$ 4·7.

Taking 3 times the probable error as a reasonable measure, we can say that when we find 5 per cent. in the sample we may write 3½ to 6½ per cent. for the whole, for 10 per cent. we may write 8 to 12 per cent., for 15 per cent. we may write 12½ to 17½ per cent., etc.,

If there is any error from the reasons discussed earlier, this is additive to the error of sampling. Thus, in Reading 20 per cent. of the working-class households are almost certainly below the standard (Table IV.[R]), another 2½ per cent. were classed as probably below, and another 2½ per cent. possibly below, so that we can only say that in the *sample* between 20 and 25 per cent. of the working-class households are below the standard. Now, adding three times the probable error we can say that in the *borough* it is practically certain that between 17 and 28 per cent. are below, but the extremes would only be reached if we had a maximum error in sampling combined with a maximum error in judgment, and I think that we may safely say " between 19 and 26 per cent."[1]

We shall not be far wrong if we affix mentally ±2 or 3 to every percentage statement for the three towns, and ±4 or 5 to those for West Stanley.

Actually we have a greater security and a smaller margin of error than this formula shows, because our samples were deliberately taken from houses distributed

---

[1] The population is a larger proportion (25 to 30 per cent.) than are the houses, since the poor houses have more than the average number of occupants.

nearly uniformly through the towns, whereas the formula applies to samples taken quite at random, as if the houses had been numbered and numbers drawn from a bag. Our distribution cannot then contain a greater number of extreme cases ; it must have a relation to the distribution of the rich, the comfortably off, the poor and the destitute, so far as these are aggregated, similar families in similar streets. We have no data for using the mathematical expression appropriate to this consideration, but it most likely reduces the margin of error sufficiently to allow us to neglect all roughnesses and unbiassed errors of record, and regard $\pm$ 2 per cent. as a very safe limit.

Where the number of cases is relatively very small (as, for example, houses in Northampton overcrowded by the Census definition), we may miss them altogether, and generally it is unsafe to rely on measurements that relate to characteristics possessed by less than say 3 or 4 per cent. in the three larger towns, and perhaps 6 per cent. in Stanley.

Where we could obtain a complete enumeration from any official statistics, we compared it with the forecast from the sample. In two cases we were able to correct the official statistics as given to us ; for, finding that they differed from the sample we made further enquiries, and found that the official statistics had been erroneously stated. In the case of school children and the most definite occupations, our sample was very near the actual numbers. Where employees of particular firms were concerned, the data were not in all cases good, and the sample less perfect—in the case of two Warrington firms very imperfect. Where we were able to compare a whole occupation (such as police) we found the forecast good.

The numbers of cases of overcrowding at the Census standard (more than 2 persons to a room) appear unduly small in the samples. This is probably due in part to a different working definition of tenement and of separate occupation, in part to the different definitions of rooms, and in part to improvement since 1911.

We did not expect to hear of all cases of out-relief; and in any case it is difficult to get comparable numbers since the unit counted may be either a person or a family.

The deficit in the number of Old-Age Pensioners is difficult to explain. Some of the absent ones may be found in shops, institutions, or better-class houses. It should be noted that there were practically no cases where people apparently over 70 were finally entered as below the poverty line, when an unrecorded Old-Age Pension would have brought them above it.

The following Table gives the comparison between the numbers obtained in the samples with their probable errors and the whole number otherwise found in the towns divided by the number (22.7, 19.3, 17.4, 21.5), which expressed the ratio of the town to the example. The names of the towns are given by initial only.

This Table helps to distinguish between the information which can be readily obtained in a house-to-house enquiry from that which needs more exhaustive methods.

	Number from Sample.	Probable Error.	Proportionate Number from Completed Records.
School Children.[1]			
N.	570	16	576 (in 1912)
W.	735	18	699
R.	623	16	632
S.	214	9	248

NOTE.—In the original Reading Report (*Stat. Journ.*, 1912-3) the standard deviation, which is $\frac{3}{2}$ of the probable error, was used in the tests.

[1] The last column refers to all public elementary school children of 5 to 14 years, and includes a small number from non-working class houses.

	Number from Sample.	Probable Error.	Proportionate Number from Completed Records.
Overcrowding (more than 2 to a room)			
N.	0	?	4
W.	15	3	40
R.	8	2	11
Houses assessed at less than £8.	about		
R.	206	8	204
N.	316	12	311
Occupations and employees of firms :—			
N.	59	5	62
	70	6	57
	51	5	44
	47	5	44
W.	131	8	131
	48	5	52
	99	7	121
	40	4	62
	36	4	52
R.	7	2	5
	8	2	9
	13	2	12
	29	4	35
	54	5	58
	185	10	230 (or less)
Old-Age Pensioners.			
N.	49	5	86
W.	25	7	41
R.	43	4	78
Out-door Relief.			
W.	22	3	34
R.	10 to 23	?	25

CONTENTS OF APPENDIX

[1] The corresponding table for Reading will be found in the *Statistical Journal*, 1912-13, pp. 697-790.

Relationship Age Occupation Employer last full week time last week full time File No.

Non-Wage Earners: Sex Age Relationship

Other Sources of Income. Enq'ry No. See over

Housing. Rent Kind of House No. of Persons No. of Rooms Garden

ACCOMMODATION OF TYPICAL HOUSES

TABLE I^N

Rent	4/6	5/6	6/6	7/6
Number of rooms ..	5	6	6	6
Height of ground floor..	8ft. 6in.	8ft 6in.	8ft. 3ft.	9ft.
Height of first floor ..	8ft. 6in.	8ft. 9in.	8ft. 6in.	8ft. 6in.
Cubic contents—	c.ft.	c. ft.	c. ft.	c. ft.
Ground floor : Front room	1,205	915	1,015	1,080
Back room	935	1,004	1,057	1,125
Living room	..	758	891	1,215
First floor : Front bedroom	1,362	1,309	1,339	1,232
Back bedroom	818	855	1,015	1,041
,, ,,	795	695	860	1,029
Total Bedrooms ..	2,975	2,859	3,214	3,302
Garden : Length ..	27ft.	42ft.	75ft.	42ft.
Breadth ..	15ft.	15ft.	18ft.	21ft.

TABLE I^W

Rent	4/6	5/3	6/6
Number of rooms	3	5	5
Height of ground floor rooms ..	8ft. 6in.	8ft. 9in.	9ft.
Av. height of first floor rooms ..	8ft. 6in.	8ft. 6in.	8ft. 9in.
Cubic contents—	c. ft.	c. ft.	c. ft.
Ground floor { Front room	1,204	1,050	1,080
Back room	..	1,113	1,386
Scullery, &c.	918	708	918
First floor { Bedroom	1,204	1,190	1,428
,, ...	995	884	1,098
,, ...	..	723	708
Total bedrooms	2,199	2,797	3,234
Yard : Area (square feet)	200	200	various

TABLE I^S

Rent	Free	Free	6/–	6/6	Free	
Number of rooms	2	3	3	4	3	
Height of rooms	9 ft.	9 ft.	9 ft.	9 ft.	9 ft.	
	Tenement House		Tenement House		Self-contained House	
	Ground Floor c. ft.	First Floor c. ft.	Ground Floor c. ft.	First Floor c. ft.	Ground Floor :	c. ft.
Bedrooms 1	1,687	1,215	1,336	1,336	Kitchen	2,896
,, 2	..	709	720	720	Scullery, etc.	567
,, 3	..	..	..	720	First floor :	
Kitchen	1,539	1,458	1,080	1,080	Bedrooms 1	1,485
Scullery, etc.	Small	Fair	486	486	,, 2	1,411
Total Bedrooms	1,687	1,924	2,056	2,776	2,896	

TABLE I^R

	4/6	5/6	6/6	7/–
Rent				
Number of rooms	4	5	5	5
Height of ground floor rooms	7ft. 9in.	7ft. 6in.	8ft. 2in.	8ft.
Average height of first floor rooms	7ft. 2in.	7ft. 9in.	8ft. 9in.	8ft.
Cubic contents—	c ft.	c ft.	c ft.	c. ft.
Ground floor :				
Front room	670	630	630	760
Back room	640	680	1,000	1,020
Scullery, &c.	0	470	640	?
First floor :				
Bedroom	685	1,135	990	1,000
,,	575	600	890	780
,,	..	1,135	740	680
Total bedrooms	1,260	2,870	2,620	2,460
Garden : Breadth	12ft.	14ft.	12ft. 6in.	12ft. 6in.
Length	36ft.	38ft.	55ft.	59ft.

EARNERS AND NON-EARNERS BY SEX AND AGE

TABLE II[N]

EARNERS.

		Per cent.
(m) Man over 20 Householder	573	19.2
Others	45	1.5
(s) Son over 20	187[1]	6.3
(s) Son 18 to 20	72[2]	2.3
(l) Lad 16 to 18	70	2.4
(b) Boy 14 to 16	51	1.7
(sc) Under 14 ..	5	.2
Total male	**1,003**	**33.6**
(w) Wife or widow ..	82	2.7
(f) Woman over 16	30	1.0
(d) Daughter over 18	198	6.7
(d) Daughter 16 to 18	54	1.8
(g) Girl 14 to 16 ..	40	1.3
Total female	**404**	**13.5**
Total earners	**1,407**	**47.2**

NON-EARNERS.

		Per cent.			Per cent.
(m) }	60	2.0	(w)	573	19.3
(s)	2		(f)	42	1.4
(l) }	6	.3	(d)	29	1.0
(b)			(g)	14	.5
(sc) School children ..				570	19.1
(in) Children under 5				278	9.3
Total non-earners				**1,574**	**52.8**
Grand total ..				**2,981**	**100**

[1] Includes 3 nephews.   [2] Includes 2 lodgers.

TABLE II^w

EARNERS

		No.	Approximate per cent.
(m)	Man over 20¹ Householders	534	17·3
	Others	86	2·8
(s)	Son over 20¹	175	5·7
(s)	Son 18 to 20¹	48	1·6
(l)	Lad 16 to 18	56	1·8
(b)	Boy 14 to 16	53	1·7
(sc)	Schoolboy	12	·4
	Total male	**964**	**31·2**
(w)	Wife or widow	48	1·6
(f)	Woman over 16	12	·4
(d)	Daughter over 18¹	111	3·6
(d)	Daughter 16 to 18¹	41	1·3
(g)	Girl 14 to 16	45	1·4
(sc)	Schoolgirl	5	·2
	Total female	**262**	**8·5**
	Total earners	**1,226**	**39·7**

NON-EARNERS

		No.	Approximate per cent.
(m) (s)	}	43	1·4
(l)	..	1	
(b)	..		·1
(sc)	School children ..	3	
(in)	Children under 5		
(w)		589	19·1
(f)		26	·9
(d)		63	2·0
(d)		12	·4
(g)		735	23·8
		391	12·7
	Total non-earners	**1,863**	**60·3**
	Grand total	**3,089**	**100**

¹ The division by age is a little uncertain in these cases.

TABLE II[s]

Category	EARNERS No.	EARNERS Approximate per cent.	NON-EARNERS No.	NON-EARNERS Approximate per cent.
(m) Man over 20 Householders	172	17·6	21	2·2
Others	32	3·3		
(s) Son 18 to 20	55	5·7	1	·1
(s) Son 16 to 18	20	2·0		
(l) Lad 16 to 18	17	1·7	1	·1
(b) Boy 14 to 16	17	1·7	5	·5
Total male	**313**	**32·1**		
(w) Wife or widow	5	·5	182	18·7
(f) Woman over 16	1	·1	13	1·3
(d) Daughter over 18	6	·6	47	4·8
(d) Daughter 16 to 18	3	·3	20	2·0
(g) Girl 14 to 16	1	·1		
(sc) School children			214	21·9
(in) Children under 5			142	14·6
Total female	**16**	**1·6**		
Total earners	**329**	**33·7**		
Total non-earners			**646**	**66·3**
Grand total			**975**	**100**

TABLE II[R].

	EARNERS.					NON-EARNERS.				
		Approximate per cent.			Approximate per cent.			Approximate per cent.			Approximate per cent.
(m) Man over 20 Householders	499[1]	19	(w) Wife or widow ..	67	2½	(m) }	} 50	} 2	(w)	449	17
Others	82	3	(f) Woman over 16 ..	32	1	(s) }			(f)	115	4
(s) Son over 20	96[2]	3	(d) Daughter over 18[2]	87	3½	(l) }	} 11	} 0.4	(d)	9	0.3
(s) Son 18 to 20[2]	41[1]	1½	(d) Daughter 16–18[2] ..	39	1½	(b) }			(d)	9	0.3
(l) Lad 16 to 18	55	2	(g) Girl 14 to 16 ..	34	1½	(sc) School children ..			(g)	623	23½
(b) Boy 14 to 16	42	1½	Girl under 14	1		(in) Children under 5				334	12½
Total male	815	30	Total female ..	260	10	Total non-earners			..	1,600	60
			Total earners ...	1,075	40	Grand total			..	2,675	100

[1] There are 11 other householders not included here for want of information as to their families.
[2] The division by age is a little uncertain in these cases.

N

In Tables III: and IV: the following abbreviations are used:—*m*, man over 18 years, distinguished as *s* (son) if living in his parents' house; *l*, lad of 16 to 18 years; *b*, boy of 14 to 16 years.

f, woman over 16 years, distinguished as *w* (wife or widow) if married, and as *d* (daughter) if living in her parents' house; *g*, girl of 14 to 16 years.

sc (scholar), boy or girl of 5 to 14 years.

in (infant), child under 5 years.

In Tables III *s* and *d* are not considered to be dependent children.

CLASSIFICATION OF 693 HOUSEHOLDS ACCORDING TO WAGE - EARNERS AND DEPENDANTS THEY CONTAIN

NORTHAMPTON

TABLE III^N

Wage-earners.	No. of households.	Dependants.
Man only	79	No children, viz., no deps., 1 ; w, 74 ; w, f, 1 ; w, d, 1 ; s, 1 ; d, s, 1.
	71	1 child, viz., w, in, 32 ; f, in, 1 ; w, sc, 28 ; w, g, 3 ; w, f, in, 1 ; w, d, sc, 1 ; w, f, b, 1 ; w, m, f, in, 3 ; d, sc, 1.
	48	2 children, viz., w, in, in, 5 ; w, sc, in, 17 ; w, sc, sc, 24 ; w, b, sc, 1 ; w, s, sc, in, 1.
	33	3 children, viz., w, in, in, in, 2 ; w, sc, in, in, 8 ; w, f, sc, in, in, 1 ; w, sc, sc, in, 12 ; f, sc, sc, in, 1 ; w, sc, sc, sc, 8 ; w, l, sc, in, 1.
	22	4 children, viz., w, sc, in, in, in, 2 ; w, sc, sc, in, in, 11 ; w, sc, sc, sc, in, 6 ; w, f, sc, sc, sc, in, 1 ; w, sc, sc, sc, sc, 1 ; w, g, sc, sc, in, 1.
	6	5 children, viz., w, sc, sc, sc, in, in, 4 ; w, sc, sc, sc, sc, in, 2.
	4	6 children, viz., w, sc, sc, sc, in, in, in, 1 ; w, sc, sc, sc, sc, sc, in, 3.
	4	7 children, viz., w, sc, sc, sc, sc, in, in, in, 2 ; w, sc, sc, sc, sc, sc, in, in, 2.
Total	267	

Wage-earners.	No. of households.	Dependants.
Man and school-boy ..	1	w, sc, sc, sc, sc, in, 1.
Man and girl	9	o, 1 ; sc, sc, 1 ; w, 1 ; w, in, 1 ; w, sc, 1 ; w, sc, in, 1 ; w, sc, sc, 1 ; w, sc, sc, sc, sc, in, 1 ; w, f, sc, sc, sc, sc, in, 1.
Man and boy ..	14	w, 2 ; w, sc, 2 ; w, sc, sc, 2 ; w, sc, sc, sc, 1 ; w, sc, sc, in, 2 ; w, sc, sc, sc, in, 2 ; w, m, 1 ; w, sc, sc, sc, sc, sc, in, 1 ; w, f, sc, 1.
Man and lad	12	o, 1 ; w, 2 ; w, sc, 2 ; w, sc, sc, 1 ; w, sc, sc, in, 1 ; w, g, sc, sc, in, 1 ; w, d, sc, sc, in, ; w, g, sc, sc, sc, in, in, in, 1 ; w, f, 1 ; g, sc, sc, 1.
Man and daughter ..	25	w, 12 ; w, sc, 2 ; w, sc, sc, 1 ; w, g, sc, 1 ; w, d, sc, 2 ; w, sc, sc, in, 1 ; w, sc, sc, in, in, 1 ; w, sc, sc, sc, in, 1 ; w, s, g, sc, sc, sc, sc, 1 ; w, f, 1 ; w, d, d, 1 ; d, 1.
Man and son	28	w, 14 ; w, sc, 2 ; w, sc, sc, 2 ; w, sc, sc, in, 1 ; w, g, sc, 1 ; w, sc, sc, sc, in, 1 ; w, sc, sc, sc, sc, 1 ; m, w, d, s, sc, sc, 1 ; w, d, 1 ; w, d, in, 1 ; w, f, 1 ; d, sc, 2.
Man, girl, and school-boy	1	w, 1.
Man, boy, and school-boy	1	w, sc, in, 1.
Man, lad, and boy ..	5	w, 1 ; w, in, 1 ; w, sc, 1 ; w, sc, in, 1 ; w, sc, sc, sc, 1.
Man, lad, and girl ..	1	w, sc, sc, sc, 1.
Man, daughter, and girl	3	w, sc, in, 1 ; w, sc, sc, in, in, 1 ; w, b, sc, sc, in, 1
Man, daughter, and boy	3	w, sc, sc, in, 1 ; w, sc, sc, sc, in, in, 1 ; sc, 1.
Man, daughter, and lad	2	w, sc, sc, 1 ; w, sc, sc, sc, in, 1.
Man, son, and girl ..	6	w, sc, 1 ; w, sc, sc, 2 ; w, sc, sc, in, 1 ; w, sc, sc, in, in, 1 ; w, sc, sc, sc, in, in, 1
Man, man, and girl ..	1	w, f, sc, 1.
Man, son, and boy ..	2	w, sc, in, 1 ; w, sc, sc, sc, in, 1.
Man, son, and lad ..	7	w, 3 ; w, sc, 1 ; w, sc, sc, 1 ; w, sc, sc, sc, 2.
Man, daughter, and daughter	13	w, 4 ; w, in, in, 1 ; w, sc, sc, 1 ; w, sc, in, in, in, 1 ; w, sc, sc, sc, sc, 1 ; w, sc, sc, sc, in, in, in, 1 ; w, b, 1 ; w, g, 1 ; w, d, 1 ; d, 1.
Man, daughter, and son	15	w, 11 ; w, sc, 1 ; w, sc, sc, 1 ; w, g, 1 ; w, s, 1.
Man, daughter, and woman	2	o, 1 ; w, 1.
Man, son, and lad ..	1	w, sc, 1.
Man and 2 sons ..	5	w, 2 ; w, sc, sc, 1 ; w, d, 2.
Man, lad, and man ..	1	w, in, in.

Wage-earners.	No. of house holds.	Dependants.
Man, son, boy, and school-boy	1	w, 1.
Man, lad, and 2 boys..	1	w, 1.
Man, son, lad and boy	2	w, sc, 1 ; w, sc, sc, sc, 1.
Man, daughter, lad and girl	1	w, 1.
Man, son, lad and girl	1	w, sc, sc, 1.
Man, son, daughter and girl	2	w, 1 ; w, sc, f, 1.
Man, son, daughter, and boy	1	o, 1.
Man, son, daughter and lad.	3	w, sc, sc, 2 ; w, d, 1.
Man, 2 sons, and lad ..	3	w, 1 ; w, sc, 1 ; w, sc, s, 1.
Man, 2 daughters and lad	3	w, in, 1 ; w, sc, sc, 1 ; w, sc, sc, sc, 1.
Man, son, lad, and woman	2	w, 1 ; w, sc, 1.
Man and 3 daughters	3	w, 2 ; w, sc, sc, in, 1.
Man, 2 sons, daughter	7	w, 4 ; w, sc, 2 ; w, m, sc, sc, 1.
Man, son and 2 daughters	5	w, 3 ; w, sc, sc, 1 ; w, sc, sc, in, in, 1.
Man and 3 sons ..	4	w, 2 ; w, in, in, 1 ; d, 1.
Man, son, daughter and woman	1	w, in, 1.
Man, son, daughter, lad and boy	1	w, sc.
Man, 2 daughters, lad and boy	1	w, sc, sc, sc, sc, 1.
Man, 2 daughters, lad and girl	1	w, sc, in, in, in, 1.
Man, 2 sons, lad and boy	1	w, sc, sc, sc, in, 1.
Man, son, 2 daughters and boy	1	w, sc, 1.
Man, son, 2 daughters and girl	1	w, s, 1.
Man, 2 daughters, son and lad	1	w, 1.
Man, 2 sons, daughter and girl	1	w, 1.
Man, 2 sons, daughter and boy	2	w, sc, 2.
Man, 2 sons, 2 daughters	4	w, 2 ; w, sc, sc, 1 ; w, s, 1.
Man, 3 sons and daughter	3	w, 2 ; w, sc, 1.
Man, 3 daughters, lad and girl	1	w, sc, 1.
Man, son, 2 daughters, lad, and boy	1	w, sc, sc, 1.

Wage-earners.	No. of households.	Dependants
Man, son, 3 daughters, and lad	1	w, sc, 1.
Man, son, 3 daughters and girl	1	w, sc, sc, 1.
Man, 2 sons, and 3 daughters	1	w, d, l, 1.
Man and 5 daughters	1	w, 1.
Man, 3 sons, daughter, lad and boy	1	w, sc, 1.
Man, 4 sons, daughter and boy	1	w, sc, sc, sc, in, 1.
Man, 3 sons, 2 daughters, lad and boy	1	w, sc, sc, in, 1.
Total	**224**	

Wage-earners.	No. of households.	Dependants
Man and wife ..	30	o, 11 ; in, 3 ; f, in, 1 ; sc, 2 ; in, in, 2 ; sc, in, 1 ; sc, sc, 5 ; sc, sc, in, 2 ; sc, sc, sc, sc, in, in, 2 ; m, f, sc, 1.
Man, wife and lad ..	1	in, 1.
Man, wife and son ..	1	o, 1.
Man, wife and daughter	3	o, 1 ; sc, 2.
Man, wife, son and daughter	1	sc, g, 1.
Man, wife and 2 daughters	2	o, 1 ; sc, sc, 1.
Man, wife, 2 daughters and boy	1	sc, sc, sc, in, 1.
Man, wife and 3 sons	1	b, 1.
Total	**40**	

Wage-earners.	No. of households.	Dependants
Man only	10	o, 2 ; w, 3 ; w, in, 1 ; w, sc, in, 1 ; w, sc, sc, 1 ; w, s, sc, 1 ; f, 1.
Woman only	1	o, 1.
Man and boy.. ..	1	w, sc, in, 1.
Man and wife.. ..	1	o, 1.
Man, son, and lad ..	1	w, 1.
Man, son and daughter	1	w, 1.
Man, 2 daughters, son and lad	1	w, 1.
Man, 2 sons, daughter	1	w, 1.
Widow, woman, 2 sons and daughter	1	o, 1.
Total	**18**	This Group " Working on own Account."

Wage-earners.	No. of households.	Dependants.
2 men	10	o, 2 ; w, 1 ; w, sc, 1 ; w, sc, in, 2 ; w, sc, in, in, 1 ; w, sc, sc, sc, in, 1 ; w, sc, sc, sc, in, in, 1 ; w, d, in, 1.
Man, man and lad ..	1	w, in, 1.
3 men	2	w, in, 1 ; w, sc, in, 1.
Man and woman ..	4	w, 1 ; f, 1 ; w, in, in, 1 ; w, sc, sc, 1.
Man and 2 women ..	4	o, 1 ; in, 1 ; sc, in, 1 ; w, sc, in, 1.
2 men and 1 woman ..	4	w, 1 ; d, 1 ; w, w, in, in, in, 1 ; w, sc, in, 1.
3 men and 2 women ..	1	o, 1.
Total	26	

One woman	15	o, 8 ; sc, 1 ; sc, sc, sc, 1 ; m, 3 ; w, 1 ; m, d, 1.
Woman and school-boy	1	o, 1.
Woman and girl ..	1	sc, 1.
Woman and daughter	3	o, 1 ; sc, 1 ; s, 1.
Woman and son ..	2	o, 2.
Woman, lad and boy	1	o, 1.
Woman, son and girl	1	sc, 1.
Woman, son and daughter	2	o, 2.
Woman, daughter, lad and boy	1	o, 1.
Woman and 3 daughters	1	m, s, sc, sc, 1.
Woman, son and 3 daughters	1	m, 1.
Woman, 2 sons, 2 daughters and boy	1	sc, 1.
3 women	1	o, 1.
Total	31	

1 girl	1	m, w, sc, 1.
1 lad	1	m, w, sc, sc, 1.
Son	17	w, 8 ; m, 2 ; m, w, 3 ; m, d, 1 ; w, f, 1 ; w, d, sc, 1 ; w, sc, sc, sc, sc, b, 1.
Daughter	6	w, 1 ; m, w, 4 ; w, d, 1.
Son and boy	1	w, sc, sc, 1.
Son and daughter ..	6	w, 5 ; m, w, 1.
2 Sons	4	w, 3 ; m, w, s, 1.
2 daughters	2	w, 1 ; w, m, 1.
Daughter, lad, girl ..	1	w, 1.
2 daughters and girl..	1	m, w, 1.
Son, daughter and girl	1	w, s, 1.
Son, daughter and lad	1	w, 1.
Son, woman and lad ..	1	m, 1.
Son and 2 daughters ..	2	m, w, 1 ; m, w. d, 1.

Wage-earners.	No. of households.	Dependants.
2 sons and daughter ..	1	w, in, 1.
3 sons	2	w, 1 ; m, w, 1.
3 daughters ..	1	w, 1.
Son, daughter, girl and lad	1	m, w, sc, 1.
3 daughters and boy..	1	m, sc, 1.
3 daughters and girl..	1	w, in, 1.
2 sons and lad ..	1	w, 1.
2 sons and 2 daughters	2	w, 1 ; w, sc, sc, 1.
Son, 2 daughters, lad and boy	2	w, d, 1, w, sc, 1.
2 sons, man and woman	1	w, in, 1.
2 sons and 3 daughters	1	w, sc, 1.
3 sons and 2 daughters	1	w, sc, sc, in, g, 1.
2 sons, 3 daughters and girl	1	w, sc, 1.
4 sons, daughter and lad	1	m, w, 1.
3 sons and 3 daughters	1	m, w, 1.
Total	63	
No earners	24	f, 12 ; f, f, 1 ; m, 2 ; m, f, 1 ; m, w, 3 ; w, sc, sc, 1 ; w, sc, in, in, 1 ; w, sc, in, in, in, 1 ; m, w, in, in, 1 ; w, d, 1.
Total	693	

CLASSIFICATION OF 640 HOUSEHOLDS, ACCORDING TO WAGE - EARNERS AND DEPENDANTS THEY CONTAIN

WARRINGTON

TABLE III^W

See note, page 194.

Wage-earners.	No. of house-holds.	Dependants.
Man only ..	.. 64	No children, viz., no dependants, 2 ; w, 60 ; w, d, 1 ; w, d, d, 1.
	66	1 child, viz., w, in, 40 ; w, sc, 19 ; w, b, 1 ; w, f, in, 1 ; w, w, in, 1 ; w, m, in, 1 ; w, f, sc, 1 ; w, d, d, sc, 2.
	59	2 children, viz., w, in, in, 21 : w, sc, in, 16 ; w, sc, sc, 17 ; w, w, sc, in, 1 ; w, d, d, sc, in, 1 ; w, d, sc, sc, 2 ; w, g, sc, 1.
	57	3 children, viz., w, in, in, in, 2 ; w, sc, in, in, 21 ; w, sc, sc, in, 23 ; w, sc, sc, sc, 8 ; f, sc, in, in, 1 ; w, m, sc, in, in, 1 ; f, sc, sc, sc, 1.
	31	4 children, viz., w, sc, in, in, in, 3 ; w, sc, sc, in, in, 12 ; w, sc, sc, sc, in, 11 ; w, sc, sc, sc, sc, 5.
	15	5 children, viz., w, sc, sc, in, in, in, 1 ; w, sc, sc, sc, in, in, 5 ; w, sc, sc, sc, sc, sc, in, 6 ; w, sc, sc, sc, sc, sc, sc, 1 ; w, w, sc, sc, sc, in, in, 1 ; w, s, d, sc, sc, sc, in, in, 1.
	5	6 children, viz., w, sc, sc, sc, in, in, in, 1 ; w, sc, sc, sc, sc, in, in, 4.
	4	7 children, viz., w, sc, sc, sc, sc, sc, in, in, in, 2 ; w, sc, sc, sc, sc, sc, sc, in, in, 2.
	301	
Man and school child	1	w, sc, in, in, 1.
Man and girl ..	.. 13	w, sc, 1 ; w, sc, in, 2 ; w, sc, sc, 2 ; w, sc, in, in, 1 ; w, sc, sc, in, 1 ; w, sc, sc, sc, 1 ; w, sc, sc, sc, in, 2 ; w, sc, sc, sc, sc, 2 ; w, sc, sc, sc, sc, sc, sc, 1.
Man and boy	.. 15	w, 1 ; w, sc, 3 ; w, sc, in, 1 ; w, d, sc, in, 1 ; w, d, sc, sc, 1 ; w, sc, sc, in, 1 ; w, sc, sc, sc, 1 ; w, sc, sc, sc, in, 2 ; w, sc, sc, sc, in, in, 1 ; w, g, sc, sc, sc, in, in, 1 ; w, sc, sc, sc, sc, in, 1 ; w, sc, sc, sc, sc, sc, in, 1.

Wage-earners.	No. of house-holds.	Dependants.
Man and lad	8	w, d, 1 ; w, in, 1 ; w, d, sc, 1 ; w, sc, in, 1 ; w, sc, sc, 1 ; f, sc, sc, 1 ; w, d, sc, sc, in, 1 ; w, m, d, sc, sc, in, 1.
Man and daughter ..	17	w, 3 ; w, d, 2 ; w, in, 2 ; w, sc, 4 ; w, d, sc, 1 ; w, g, sc, 1 ; w, sc, sc, sc, 1 ; w, d, sc, sc, sc, sc, 1 ; w, g, sc, sc, in, in, 1 ; w, sc, sc, sc, sc, sc, in, 1.
Man and son	19	w, 7 ; w, d, 3 ; w, s, d, 1 ; w, sc, 1 ; w, l, sc, in, 1 ; w, d, sc, in, 1 ; w, sc, sc, 1 ; w, d, sc, sc, 1 ; w, d, sc, sc, sc, 1 ; w, d, d, sc, in, in, in, 1 ; w, sc, sc, sc, in, 1.
Man, boy and school-boy	2	w, sc, sc, in, in, 1 ; w, sc, sc, sc, in, 1.
Man, girl and school-child	2	w, sc, 1 ; w, sc, sc, sc, in, 1.
Man and 2 girls ..	1	w, sc, sc, 1.
Man, lad and boy ..	2	sc, 1 ; w, sc, sc, sc, 1.
Man, lad and girl ..	4	w, 2 ; w, sc, in, in, 1 ; w, sc, sc, sc, in, 1.
Man, daughter and girl	3	w, sc, 1 ; w, sc, in, 1 ; w, sc, sc, 1.
Man, daughter and school child	1	w, sc, sc, sc, in, 1.
Man, daughter and boy	5	w, d, 1 ; w, d, sc, in, 1 ; w, d, sc, sc, 1 ; w, sc, sc, sc, in, in, 1 ; w, sc, sc, sc, sc, sc, 1.
Man, daughter and lad	3	w, 1 ; w, sc, sc, 2.
Man, son and school-boy	2	w, d, sc, 1 ; w, sc, sc, sc, 1.
Man, son and boy ..	4	w, sc, in, 2 ; w, d, sc, sc, sc, sc, sc, 1 ; w, d, sc, 1.
Man, son and girl ..	1	w, d, sc, sc, in, 1.
Man, son and lad ..	5	w, 1 ; w, d, 1 ; w, g, sc, 1 ; w, sc, sc, sc, sc, 1 ; w, sc, sc, sc, sc, sc, in, 1.
Man and 2 daughters	4	None, 1 ; w, d, 1 ; w, w, 1 ; m, w, w, 1.
Man, son and daughter	12	w, 7 ; w, d, 1 ; w, sc, sc, 1 ; w, sc, sc, in, 1 ; w, sc, sc, sc, 1 ; w, g, sc, sc, in, 1.
Man and 2 sons ..	7	w, 4 ; w, sc, sc, 1 ; w, g, sc, sc, 1 ; w, g, sc, sc, sc, sc, in, 1.
Man, lad, girl and school-boy	1	w, sc, sc, sc, in, in, 1.
Man, daughter, lad and school-girl	1	w, sc, sc, 1.
Man, daughter, lad and boy	3	w, 1 ; w, sc, 1 ; w, w, sc, sc, sc, in, 1.
Man, son, daughter and school-boy	1	w, sc, sc, sc, sc, in, in, 1.
Man, son, daughter, and boy	3	w, d, d, sc, sc, 1 ; w, sc, sc, sc, sc, sc, 1 ; w, sc, sc, 1.
Man, son, daughter and girl	5	w, sc, 1 ; w, g, 1 ; w, sc, sc, 1 ; w, sc, sc, in, in, 1 ; d, sc, sc, sc, sc, 1.
Man, son, daughter and lad	1	w, sc, 1.

Wage-earners.	No. of house-holds.	Dependants.
Man, 2 sons and boy	1	w, d, d, sc, sc, 1.
Man, 2 sons and lad..	3	w, 2 ; w, sc, sc, 1.
Man, 2 daughters and boy	2	w, 1 ; w, in, 1.
Man, 2 daughters and son	2	w, 1 ; w, sc, 1.
Man, 2 sons and daughter	3	w, 1 ; w, sc, sc, sc, sc, in, 1 ; w, sc, sc, sc, sc, in, in, 1.
Man and 3 sons ..	1	w, sc, 1.
Man, son, daughter, lad and boy	1	w, sc, sc, sc, 1.
Man, 2 sons, lad and girl	1	w, d, sc, sc, in, in, 1.
Man, 2 daughters, lad and boy	3	w, 1 ; w, in, 1 ; w, sc, in, 1.
Man, 2 sons, daughter and girl	2	w, s, 1 ; w, sc, sc, sc, 1.
Man, 3 sons and boy	1	w, sc, sc, sc, sc, sc, sc, 1.
Man, 3 sons and lad..	1	w, 1.
Man, 2 sons and 2 daughters	1	w, 1.
Man, son and 3 daughters	2	w, d, 1 ; w, sc, sc, in, 1.
Man, 3 sons and daughter	1	w, g, sc, sc, sc, 1.
Man and 4 sons ..	2	w, sc, sc, 1 ; w, sc, sc, sc, in, in, 1.
Man, 3 sons, 2 daughters and school-girl	1	w, sc, sc, in, 1.
Man, 2 sons and 4 daughters	1	w, sc, sc, 1.
Total ..	..175	

Man and wife ..	14	d, 1 ; in, 1 ; f, sc, 1 ; w, sc, 1 ; in, in, 1 ; sc, sc, 3 ; sc, sc, sc, 2 ; sc, sc, sc, in, 2 ; sc, sc, sc, sc, sc, 1 ; sc, sc, sc, sc, in, in, 1.
Man, wife and school child	1	sc, in, 1.
Man, wife and girl ..	1	sc, in, 1.
Man, wife and 2 sons	1	sc, sc, sc, 1.
Man, wife, son, daughter and girl	1	sc, in, 1.
Man, wife, son, boy and 2 school children	1	sc, sc, in, in, in, 1.
Man, wife and 3 daughters	1	sc, sc, 1.

Wage-earners.	No. of households.	Dependants.
Man	7	w, 1 ; w, sc, in, 2 ; w, sc, in, in, 1 ; w, g, sc, in, 1 ; w, sc, sc, sc, in, 1 ; f, f, f, f, f, f, 1.
Wife	1	m, 1.
Man and wife ..	1	d, sc, sc, in, 1.
Widow and 2 men ..	1	None, 1.
Man and girl	1	w, 1.
Man and son	2	w, 2.
Man, wife, son and woman	1	None, 1.
Man and 3 sons ..	1	d, 1.
2 men, son, lad, and 2 daughters	1	b, in, w, 1.
	16	This group "working on own account."

Two men	10	w, d, 1 ; w, m, 1 ; w, d, in, 1 ; w, sc, 2 ; w, in, in, 1 ; w, sc, sc, 1 ; w, w, sc, sc, in, 1 ; w, f, sc, sc, sc, 1 ; w, sc, sc, sc, in, 1.
Man and woman ..	2	f, 1 ; w, w, sc, sc, sc, in, 1.
Two men and boy ..	1	w, f, sc, sc, sc, in, in, in, 1.
2 men and son ..	1	w, d, 1.
2 men and daughter..	2	w, 1 ; w, sc, in, 1.
2 men and woman ..	3	f, 1 ; w, in, 1 ; w, sc, 1.
2 men and wife ..	1	w, d, sc, in, 1.
3 men	1	w, m, 1.
2 men and 2 sons ..	1	w, d, sc, sc, in, 1.
2 men and wife ..	1	w, in, 1.
Man, wife, and widow	1	sc, 1.
2 men, wife, 2 sons and 3 daughters	1	None, 1.
	25	

1 woman	3	m, f, 1 ; f, f, f, 1 ; sc, sc, 1.
Woman and lad ..	3	None, 1 ; s, 1 ; m, f, sc, sc, 1.
Woman and daughter	2	None, 1 ; m, sc, sc, sc, sc, 1.
Woman and son ..	2	None, 1 ; m, sc, in, 1.
Woman, lad and boy	2	None, 1 ; sc, sc, sc, sc, in, 1.
Woman and 2 daughters	1	None, 1.
Woman, son, 2 daughters and girl	1	m, 1.
Woman, son and 2 daughters	1	s, 1.
Woman, 2 sons, girl and school child	1	None, 1.
Woman, 3 sons and school child	1	m, 1.
	17	

Wage-earners.	No. of households.	Dependants.
Girl	2	m, w, sc, in, in, 1 ; w, sc, sc, sc, in, in, 1.
Boy	2	w, sc, in, 1 ; w, d, sc, 1.
Lad	1	w, 1.
Daughter	3	w, 1 ; m, w, 2.
Son	19	w, 9 ; m, w, 4 ; d, m, 1 ; w, d, 1 ; m, w, d, 1 ; w, w, in, 1 ; m, d, in, 1 ; w, m, sc, sc, in, 1.
Daughter and girl	1	w, sc, 1.
Son and lad	3	w, 1 ; w, d, 1 ; m, w, sc, 1.
Son and daughter	8	w, 8.
Two sons	3	w, 2 ; w, sc, 1.
Two daughters	1	w, 1.
Son, lad and boy	1	w, sc, sc, 1.
Son, daughter and boy	1	w, w, sc, sc, in, 1.
Son, lad and daughter	1	w, 1.
2 sons and lad	1	w, 1.
Son, lad and girl	1	w, sc, 1.
Daughter and 2 girls	1	w, sc, 1.
3 daughters	1	w, 1.
3 sons	1	w, 1.
2 sons and daughter	6	w, 5 ; w, s, 1.
Son and 2 daughters	1	m, 1.
2 sons, lad and boy	1	w, 1.
Son, daughter, lad and boy	1	w, sc, sc, in, 1.
3 sons and lad	2	w, 1 ; w, sc, sc, 1.
3 sons and daughter	1	w, 1.
Son and 3 daughters	1	w, sc, in, in, 1.
4 sons	1	w, d, 1.
4 sons and boy	1	m, w, 1.
Son, 2 daughters, lad and man	1	w, d, s, 1.

67

| No earners] | 19 | w, 6 ; f, 3 ; m, d, 1 ; m, w, 3 ; f, f, 1 ; w, sc, 1 ; m, w, sc, 1 ; w, m, sc, in, 1 ; m, w, sc, sc, in, 1 ; m, w, g, sc, sc, 1. |
| Total | | 640 |

CLASSIFICATION OF 203 HOUSEHOLDS ACCORDING TO WAGE - EARNERS AND DEPENDANTS THEY CONTAIN

STANLEY

TABLE III[s]

See note, page 194.

Wage-earners.	No. of house-holds.	Dependants.
Man only	24	No children, viz., w, 15 ; f, 4 ; d, 1 ; w, m, 1 ; w, d, 1 ; w, f, 1 ; d, d, 1.
	35	1 child, viz., w, in, 26 ; w, sc, 8 ; w, b, 1.
	25	2 children, viz., w, in, in, 7 ; w, sc, in, 15 ; w, sc, sc, 1 ; w, in, in, f, 1 ; w, d, g, sc, 1.
	20	3 children, viz., w, in, in, in, 3 ; w, sc, in, in, 4 ; w, sc, sc, in, 8 ; w, sc, sc, sc, 2 ; w, g, sc, sc, 1 ; w, sc, in, in, f, 1 ; w, sc, sc, in, f, 1.
	6	4 children, viz., w, sc, sc, in, in, 2 ; w, sc, sc, in, 1 ; w, sc, sc, sc, sc, 1 ; w, d, sc, sc, in, in, 1 ; w, m, sc, sc, sc, sc, 1.
	7	5 children, viz., w, sc, sc, sc, in, in, 3 ; w, sc, sc, sc, sc, in, 1 ; w, sc, sc, sc, sc, sc, 1 ; w, g, sc, 3, sc, sc, in, 2.
	2	6 children, viz., w, g, sc, sc, sc, in, in, 2.
	1	7 children, viz., w, g, sc, sc, sc, sc, in, in, 1.
	120	
Man and boy ..	4	w, 1 ; w, d, g, s, sc, in, 1 ; w, sc, sc, sc, sc, in, in, 1 ; w, b, sc, sc, sc, sc, in, in, 1.
Man and lad	6	w, 2 ; w, g, in, 1 ; w, d, d, in, 1 ; w, g, sc, sc, 1 ; w, sc, sc, sc, sc, 1.
Man and daughter ..	2	w, 1 ; w, g, sc, sc, sc, in, 1.
Man and son	13	w, 1 ; w, g, sc, 1 ; w, d, d, sc, in, 1 ; w, d, sc, in, in, 1 ; w, d, g, sc, sc, 1 ; w, d, d, sc, sc, sc, 1 ; w, sc, sc, sc, in, in, 1 ; w, g, sc, sc, sc, in, 1 ; w, d, 2 ; w, d, d, 1 ; f 2.
Man, lad and boy ..	1	w, sc, sc, sc, sc, in, 1.
Man, son and boy ..	1	w, d, sc, 1.
Man, son and daughter	3	w, d, d, l, 1 ; w, sc, sc, sc, 1 ; w, sc, sc, sc, in, in, 1.
Man and 2 sons ..	2	w, d, in, 1 ; w, sc, sc, sc, 1.
Man, 2 sons and boy ..	2	w, sc, sc, 1 ; w, d, sc, sc, in, in, 1.
Man, 2 sons and lad ..	3	w, g, 1 ; w, d, g, 1 ; d, d, sc, sc, 1.
Man and 3 sons ..	3	w, m, sc, 1 ; w, sc, sc, sc, 1 ; w, g, sc, sc, 1.

Wage-earners.	No. of households.	Dependants.
Man, 3 sons and boy	1	w, d, sc, 1.
Man and 4 sons ..	1	w, d, b, 1.
Man, son and 3 daughters	1	w, g, sc, sc, 1.
Man, 4 sons and boy..	1	w, d, d, sc, sc, sc, 1.
	44	
Man and woman ..	2	f, 1 ; b, sc, 1.
Man (working on own account)	1	w, sc, sc, 1.
2 men	2	None, 1 ; w, sc, sc, sc, 1.
2 men and son ..	1	w, d, d, b, 1.
3 men and son ..	1	d, d, sc, in, 1.
4 men	1	f, 1.
	5	
1 woman	1	d, 1.
Woman and boy ..	1	m, sc, sc, sc, in, 1.
Woman and son ..	1	m, d, 1.
Woman, lad and girl	1	m, sc, sc, sc, sc, sc, in, 1.
	4	
Boy	1	m, w, sc, sc, sc, sc, 1.
Daughter	1	m, w, 1.
Son	3	w, 1 ; m, d, 1 ; w, g, sc, 1.
Lad and boy ..	1	w, d, sc, 1.
Son and boy ..	1	w, sc, sc, sc, in, in, 1.
Son and lad ..	2	m, w, d, 1 ; w, sc, sc, 1.
2 sons	3	m, w, 2 ; m, d, d, 1.
2 sons and boy ..	1	w, d, d, 1.
3 sons and lad ..	1	m, w, d, sc, 1.
3 sons, lad and boy ..	1	w, d, d, sc, sc, sc, sc, 1.
	15	
No earners	12	w, 2 ; m, w, 2 ; m, f, 1 ; w, sc, 1 ; m, w, sc, 1 ; w, sc, in, 1 ; m, w, sc, sc, 1 ; w, in, in, in, 1 ; m, w, sc, sc, sc, in, 1; m,w, sc, sc, in, in, in, 1.
	203	

CLASSIFICATION OF HOUSEHOLDS ACCORDING TO EARNERS AND THE MINIMUM STANDARD

In Tables IV[N], IV[W], IV[S], and IV[R], in the first column, dependent children are included whatever their age. The number over 14 years is very small.

The abbreviations are explained on p. 194.

TABLE IV[N]

(1) = Number of Dependent Children.
(2) = Number of Households.
(3) = Below New Standard.
(4) = Probably below Standard.
(5) = Possibly below Standard.
(6) = Deficiency from New Standard of those classed as below (nearest shilling). The letters f, m, &c., show dependants other than children.

		[1]	[2]	[3]	[4]	[5]	[6]
1 man earning		0	76	3[1]	..	..	1, 1, 1
		1	71	..	..	..	
		2	50	1	1	..	1
		3	33	6[2]	..	..	3, 3, 1, 1, 1, 1,
		4	23	5[2]	..	..	6, 3, 2, 1, 1
		5	6	1	..	1	8
		6	4	3	..	..	4, 4, 3
		7	4	2	..	..	8, 4
Totals	..		267	21	1	1	
Man and 1 son		0	37	..	..	..	
or daughter		1	13	1	..	..	3
earning		2	17	..	..	..	
		3	7	1	..	..	4[4]
		4	9	1	..	..	3
		5	3	2	..	..	1 (f), 2
		6	2	1	..	..	6
		7	1	1	..	..	6
Totals	..		89	7	..	..	

TABLE IV*—*Continued.*

	(1)	(2)	(3)	(4)	(5)	(6)
I man and 2 sons or daughters earning	0	24	..	..	..	
	1	15	..	..	..	
	2	14	..	..	..	
	3	6	..	..	..	
	4	8	0²	..	..	
	5	1	1	..	..	1
	6	1	..	..	..	
Totals ...		69	1	..	..	
I man and 3 sons or daughters earning	0	18	1	..	..	5
	1	11	..	..	..	
	2	7	..	..	..	
	3	3	..	..	..	
	4	1	..	..	..	
Totals		40	1	..	..	
I man and 4 sons or daughters earning	0	6	..	..	..	(Up to this point the wife is at home, not earning, in *all* cases below standard)
	1	7	..	..	..	
	2	1	..	..	..	
	4	3	..	..	..	
Totals ...		17	..	..	..	
I man and 5 sons or daughters earning	0	1	..	..	..	
	1	2	..	..	..	
	2	3	..	..	..	
Totals ..		6	..	..	..	
I man and 6 sons or daughters earning	1	1	..	..	..	
	4	1	..	..	..	
Totals ..		2	..	..	..	
I man and 7 sons or daughters earning	3	1	..	..	..	
Totals ..		1	..	..	..	

TABLE IV^B—*Continued.*

	(1)	(2)	(3)	(4)	(5)	(6)
Man and wife earning	0	11	1	..	..	4
	1	7	..	..	..	
	2	8	1	..	..	2
	3	2	..	..	..	
	6	2	1^s	..	..	3
Totals ..		30	3	..	..	
Man, wife and 1 son or daughter earning	0	2	..	..	..	
	1	3	..	..	..	
Totals ..		5	..	..	..	
Man, wife and 2 sons or daughters earning	0	1	..	..	..	
	2	2	..	..	..	
Totals ...		3	..	..	..	
Man, wife and 3 sons or daughters earning	1	1	..	..	..	
	4	1	..	..	..	
Totals ..		2	..	..	..	
1 or more persons working on their own account	0	13	..	..	2	
	1	1	..	..	..	
	2	4	...	..	1	
Totals ...		18	..	..	3	
Misc. groups of earners containing at least 1 man	0	8	..	..	..	
	1	5	..	..	..	
	2	9	..	..	..	
	3	2	..	..	..	
	4	1	..	..	..	
	5	1	...	..	...	
Totals ..		26	..	..	..	

o

TABLE IV^N—*Continued.*

	(1)	(2)	(3)	(4)	(5)	(6)
1 woman earning	0	10	4	1	1	1, no dependants, 9⁴, 10⁴, m, 4, m.
	1	2	1	..	..	
	2	2	..	..	..	
	3	1	..	..	..	
Totals ..		15	5	1	1	
1 woman and 1 son or daughter earning	0	4	1	..	..	7
	1	3	1	..	1	3
Totals ..		7	2	..	1	
1 woman and 2 or more sons and daughters earning	0	5	..	..	..	
	1	2	..	..	..	
	3	1	1	..	..	4, m.
Totals ..		8	1	..	..	
3 women earning	0	1	..	..	..	
Sons and daughters only earning	0	42	1	..	2	3⁴, m, w
	1	15	1	..	..	6, g earning, m, w, sc, dep.
	2	4	..	..	..	
	4	1	..	..	..	
	5	1	1	..	..	9⁴, s working, w, sc, sc, sc, sc, sc, dependent
Totals ..		63	3	..	2	
No apparent earners	0	19	5	2	5	?⁴, w; ?⁴, f; 2, f; ?, m, w; ?⁴, w.
	1	1	..	..	..	
	2	2	2	..	..	?⁴, w; ?, m, w.
	3	1	2	..	..	1 (w); ?⁴, w.
	4	1	1	..	..	
Totals		24	9	2	5	

TABLE IV*—*Continued.*

	(2)	(3)	(4)	(5)
Grand Totals	693	..	4	13
Below Mr. Rowntree's Standard	..	57	..	..
Below New Standard	..	53	..	..

[1] Two of the cases in each of the groups thus marked are below the New Standard, but above Mr. Rowntree's.

[2] Two additional cases in each of the groups thus marked are below Mr. Rowntree's Standard, but above the New Standard.

[3] One additional case in these groups is below Mr. Rowntree's, though above the New, Standard.

[4] Poor Relief stated in 10 cases.

TABLE IV[w]

See notes pp. 194 and 207.

(1) = No. of Dependent Children.
(2) = No. of Households.
(3) = Below New Standard.
(4) = Probably below Standard.
(5) = Possibly below Standard.
(6) = Deficiency from New Standard of those classed as below (nearest shilling). The letters f, m, etc., show dependants other than children.

	(1)	(2)	(3)	(4)	(5)	(6)
Man only ..	0	62	...	..	...	
	1	66	2	..	..	3 (w), 4
	2	57	3[1]	..	...	1, 1, 1
	3	60	10[2]	..	..	1, 1, 1, 1 (f), 2, 2, 2, 2 (f), 3, 4
	4	32	15	2	..	1, 1, 1, 2, 2, 2, 2, 3, 3, 3, 4, 4, 4, 5, 6
	5	14	9[2]	..	..	3, 3, 4, 4, 4, 6, 6, 7, 8
	6	6	4	..	..	5, 6, 9, 11
	7	4	2[1]	..	..	2, 7
Totals ..		301	45	2	..	
I man and I son or daughter earning	0	14	..	..	..	
	1	15	..	..	..	
	2	14	..	1	..	
	3	11	2[2]	..	..	1, 3
	4	10	1	..	..	6
	5	4	3	..	..	2, 5, 6
	6	5	3	..	..	8, 8, 10
Totals ..		73	9	1	..	
I man and 2 sons or daughters earning	0	18	..	..	..	
	1	7	..	..	..	
	2	12	..	..	..	
	3	8	1	..	..	3
	4	7	2[2]	..	..	1, 1
	5	3	2	..	..	3, 3
	6	3	..	..	..	
Totals ..		58	5	..	..	

TABLE IVw—*Continued.*

	[1]	(2)	[3]	(4)	(5)	(6)
1 man and 3 sons or daughters earning	0	6	1	..	..	6
	1	7	..	..	..	
	2	4	..	..	..	
	4	5	..	..	..	
	5	3	..	..	..	
	6	2	..	..	..	
Totals ..		27	1	..	..	
1 man and 4 sons or daughters earning	0	3	..	..	..	Up to this point the wife is at home, not earning, in all cases below the standard but one.
	1	3	..	..	..	
	2	2	..	..	..	
	3	3	..	..	..	
	4	1	..	..	..	
	5	2	..	..	..	
	6	1	..	..	..	
Totals ..		15	..	..	..	
1 man and 6 sons or daughters earning	2	1	..	..	..	
	3	1	..	..	..	
Totals ..		2	..	..	..	
Man and wife earning	0	0	..	..	..	
	1	4	..	..	..	
	2	4	..	..	..	
	3	2	1	..	..	3
	4	2	1	..	..	6
	5	1	1	..	..	3
	6	1	..	..	..	
Totals		14	3	..	..	
Man, wife and 1 or more children earning	2	4	1	..	..	?
	3	1	..	..	..	
	5	1	..	..	..	
Totals ..		6	1	..	..	

TABLE IV^{w}—*Continued*.

	(1)	(2)	(3)	(4)	(5)	(6)
1 or more men and others working on their own account	0 1 2 3 4	8 1 3 2 2	.. ..	 2	.. .. .. 1 ..	
Totals ..		16	..	2	1	
Miscellaneous groups of earners containing at least 1 man	0 1 2 3 4 6	6 8 4 4 2 1	.. ..	.. ..	.. ..	
Totals ..		25	..	..	..	
1 woman earning	0 2	2 1	1 ..	.. ..	.. ..	? (m, f)
Totals ..		3	1	..	..	
1 woman and 1 son or daughter earning	0 1 2 4	3 1 2 1	.. 1^3 .. 1	.. .. 1 ..	.. ..	 1 11 (m)
Totals ..		7	2	1	..	
1 woman and 2 or more sons and daughters earning	0 1 5	4 2 1	.. .. ..	 1	.. .. ..	
Totals ..		7	..	1	..	
Sons and daughters only earning	0 1 2 3 5	43 12 6 5 1	1 2^3 1 1 1	.. ..	.. ..	5 1, 2 5 ? (m) 7
Totals ..		67	6	..	..	

TABLE IV^W—*Continued*.

	(1)	(2)	(3)	(4)	(5)	(6)
No apparent earnings	0	6[4]	..	..	..	
	1	1	..	..	..	
	2	1	..	..	..	
	3	1	..	1	..	
Totals ..		9	..	1	..	
Past work	0	7	1	..	..	1
	1	2	...	..	..	
	3	1	...	..	..	
Totals ...		10	1	..	..	
Grand Totals		640	..	8	1	
Below Mr. Rowntree's Standard		..	78	..	..	
Below New Standard		..	74	..	..	

[1] Also one additional case below Mr. Rowntree's Standard.

[2] Also three additional cases in each group below Mr. Rowntree's Standard.

[3] One case in each group thus marked is above Mr. Rowntree's, though below the New Standard.

[4] These are six cases of women letting lodgings or apartments.

TABLE IV⁸

See notes pp. 194 and 207.

(1) = Number of Dependent Children.
(2) = Number of Households.
(3) = Below New Standard.
(4) = Possibly below Standard.
(5) = Deficiency from New Standard of those classed as below (nearest shilling). The letters f, m, etc., show dependants other than children.

	(1)	(2)	(3)	(4)	(5)
1 man earning	0	21	..	..	
	1	38	..	..	
	2	24	..	..	
	3	21	..	..	
	4	5	..	..	
	5	8	2	..	1, 8
	6	2	..	..	
	7	1	..	..	Wife at home,
Totals ..		120	2	..	not earning, in both cases.
1 man and 1 son or daughter earning	0	7	..	..	
	1	2	..	..	
	2	3	..	..	
	3	2	..	..	
	4	4	..	..	
	5	5	..	1	
	6	1	..	..	
	7	1	..	..	
Totals ..		25	..	1	
1 man and 2 sons or daughters earning ..	2	2	..	..	
	3	3	..	..	
	5	1	..	..	
	6	1	..	..	
Total		7	..	..	
1 man and 3 sons or daughters earning	1	2	..	..	
	2	2	..	..	
	3	2	..	..	
	4	1	..	..	
	5	1	..	..	
Total ..		8	..	..	

TABLE IV^s—*Continued.*

	(1)	(2)	(3)	(4)	(5)
1 man and 4 sons or daughters earning	2 3	2 1	.. ..	.. ..	
Total ..		3	..	..	
1 man and 5 sons or daughters earning	5	1	..	..	
Man and wife earning	2	1	..	..	
1 man working on his own account	2	1	..	..	
Miscellaneous groups of earners containing at least 1 man	0 3 4	3 2 1	1	.. .. ..	3 (f)
Total ..		6	1	..	
1 woman earning	1	1	1	..	6
1 woman and 1 son earning..	1 4	1 1	.. 1	.. ..	14 (m)
Totals ..		2	1	..	
1 woman and 2 sons or daughters earning	6	1	1	..	11 (m)
Sons and daughters only earning	0 1 2 4 5 6	4 2 6 1 1¹ 1	.. .. .. 1	.. ..	3 (m)
Totals ..		15	1	..	

TABLE IV^s—*Continued.*

	(1)	(2)	(3)	(4)	(5)
No apparent earnings	0	2	1	..	3
	1	1	..	..	
	2	1	..	..	(m)
	4	1	1	..	(m)
	5	1	1	..	
Totals ..		6²	3	..	
Past work	0	3	1	..	10 (m)
	1	1	..	..	
	2	1	..	..	
	3	1	..	..	
Totals ..		6³	1	..	
Grand totals		203	..	1	
Below Mr. Rowntree's Standard			12	..	
Below New Standard			11	..	

¹ Below Mr. Rowntree's but above New Standard.

² Two of these cases are women keeping lodgers, one other being widow of man killed in mine.

³ Three of these cases are where man has received injuries in the mine and in one the man is in a sanatorium.

TABLE IV[R]

See notes pp. 124 and 207.

(1) = Number of Dependent Children.
(2) = Number of Households.
(3) = Below New Standard.
(4) = Probably below Standard.
(5) = Possibly below Standard.
(6) = Deficiency from New Standard of those classed as below (nearest shilling). The letters f, m, &c., show dependants other than children.

	(1)	(2)	(3)	(4)	(5)	(6)
I man earning	0	65	2	..	..	2, 7 (m, f)
	1	69	2	..	..	2, 2
	2	58	15[1]	2	2	1, 1, 1, 2, 2, 2, 2, 3, 3, 3, 4, 5, 5, 5 (f), 6 (f)
	3	36	16	..	2	1, 2, 2, 2, 2, 3, 3, 3, 4, 4, 5, 5, 5, 6, 11 (f), 12
	4	23	15[2]	1	1	1, 2, 2, 2, 3, 3, 5, 6, 6, 7, 7, 7, 7, 8, 12
	5	12	8	2	..	3, 4, 5, 6, 7, 7, 8, 9
	6	9	6	2	..	5, 6, 6, 8, 11, 12
	7	6	3	3	..	8, 12, 18
	8	1	1	..	..	1
	?	11	1	3	..	
Totals ..		290	69	13	5	
I man and I son	0	35	..	..	..	
or daughter	1	9	1[4]	..	..	1 (f)
earning	2	10	..	..	..	
	3	18	3[2]	..	..	4, 7 (f), 24
	4	5	5	..	..	2, 3, 4, 4, 6
	5	2	2	..	..	2, 3
	6	1	1	..	..	1
Totals ..		80	12	..	..	
I man and 2 sons	0	20	..	..	..	
or daughters	1	12	..	..	..	
earning	2	9	..	..	..	
	3	6	1[4]	..	..	1
	4	6	2[4]	..	..	2, 3
	5	3	..	..	..	
	6	3	3	..	..	4, 16, 20
Totals		59	6	..	..	

TABLE IV^R—*Continued*.

	(1)	(2)	(3)	(4)	(5)	(6)
I man and 3 sons or daughters earning	0	6	..	..	..	Up to this point the wife is at home, and not earning, in every family below the standard except one (the second).
	1	5	..	..	..	
	2	3	..	..	..	
	3	2	..	..	..	
	4	1	..	..	..	
	5	2	..	..	..	
Totals ..		19	..	..	..	
I man and 4 sons or daughters earning	0	1	..	..	..	
	2	2	..	..	..	
	4	1	..	..	..	
Totals ..		4	..	..	..	
Man and wife earning	0	7	..	..	..	
	1	3	..	..	..	
	2	6	1	..	..	11
	3	3	..	..	..	
	4	1	..	..	..	
Totals ..		20	1	..	..	
Man, wife, and 1 son or daughter earning	0	4	..	..	..	
	1	3	..	1	..	
	3	1	..	..	..	
	4	1	..	1	..	
Totals ..		9	..	2	..	
Man, wife, and 2 3, or 4 sons and daughters earning	2	3	..	..	..	
	3	3	..	..	..	
	4	1	..	..	..	
Totals ..		7	..	..	..	
I or more men and others working on their own account	0	5	..	..	1	
	1	1	1	..	..	8 (m, w, s, d working, b dependent).
	2	4	1	..	1	3 (m working, w, in, in, dependent).
	3	2	..	..	..	
	7	1	1	..	..	11 (m working, w and 7 children dependent).
Totals ..		13	3	..	2	

TABLE IVR—*Continued.*

	(1)	(2)	(3)	(4)	(5)	(6)
Miscellaneous groups of earners containing at least one man	0	10	..	..	..	
	1	2	..	..	..	
	2	5	1	..	..	8 (m, l, f, g working, m, f, sc, sc, dependent).
	3	1	..	..	..	
	4	1	..	..	..	
Totals ..		19	1	..	..	
1 woman earning	0	21	6	..	3	2, 2, 4, no dependants, and 4, 5,² 10,² m dependent.
	1	3	2	..	..	4, 5
	4	1	1	..	..	16² (m dependent).
	5	1	1	..	..	18 (m dependent).
Totals ...		26	10	..	3	
1 woman and 1 son or daughter earning	0	6	1	..	1	4 (w, b working, no dependants).
	1	3	1	..	..	9 (w, b working).
	3	1	1	..	..	17² (w, b working).
	4	1	1	..	..	15 (w, b working, m dependent).
Totals ..		11	4	..	1	
1 woman and 2 or more sons and daughters earning	0	8	3⁴	..	..	2 (w, s, d working, m. dependent); 4 (w, b, b working, no dependants); 3 (w, d, g working, no dependants).
	1	2	..	..	..	
	2	1	1	..	..	7 (w, d, b working, m dependent).
	3	1	1	..	..	5 (w, d, d, b working).
Totals ..		12	5	..	..	
Sons and daughters only earning	0	9	..	..	..	
	1	6	1	..	..	9 (d working, f dependent).
	2	2	2	..	..	10² (d, d, g working, f dependent); 10 (s, d, g working, f dependent)
	5	1	1	..	..	12 (s, s, b, b working, m, f dependent).
Totals ..		18	4	..	..	

TABLE IVʀ—*Continued.*

	(1)	(2)	(3)	(4)	(5)	(6)
No apparent earnings	0	2	2	..	..	3 (f), 6[2] (f)
	1	1	1	..	..	10 (f)
	2	1	..	1	..	
	4	3	1	1	1	18 (f)
Totals ..		7	4	2	1	
Past work	0	26	7[2]	..	5	1 (m, f), 1 (m, f), 10[2] (m, f), 2 (f), 4 (f), 11[2] (f), ? (f)
	1	2	1	..	..	4 (m, f)
Totals ..		28	8	..	5	
Grand totals ..		622	..	17	17	
Below Mr. Rowntree's standard		..	128	..	..	
Below new standard		..	127	..	..	

[1] Also two additional cases below Mr. Rowntree's Standard only.

[2] Also one additional case below Mr. Rowntree's Standard only.

[3] Poor relief stated in these cases.

[4] One case in each of the four groups thus marked is above Mr. Rowntree's, though below the New Standard.

The List of Titles
in the Garland Series

9. Edward Cadbury, M. Cécile Matheson and George Shann. **Women's Work and Wages.** London, 1906.

10. Arnold Freeman. **Boy Life and Labour. The Manufacture of Inefficiency.** London, 1914.

11. Edward G. Howarth and Mona Wilson. **West Ham. A Study in Social and Industrial Problems.** London, 1907.

12. B.L. Hutchins. **Women in Modern Industry.** London, 1915.

13. M. Loane. **From Their Point of View.** London, 1908.

14. J. Ramsay Macdonald. **Women in the Printing Trades. A Sociological Study.** London, 1904.

15. C.F.G. Masterman. **From the Abyss. Of Its Inhabitants by One of Them.** London, 1902.

16. L.C. Chiozza Money. **Riches and Poverty.** London, 1906.

17. Richard Mudie-Smith, Ed. **Handbook of the "Daily News" Sweated Industries' Exhibition.** London, 1906.

18. Edward Abbott Parry. **The Law and the Poor.** London, 1914.

19. Alexander Paterson. **Across the Bridges. Or Life by the South London River-side.** London, 1911.

20. M.S. Pember-Reeves. **Round About a Pound a Week.** London, 1913.

21. B. Seebohm Rowntree. **Poverty. A Study of Town Life.** London, 1910 (2nd ed.).

2. B. Seebohm Rowntree and Bruno Lasker. **Unemployment. A Social Study.** London, 1911.

3. B. Seebohm Rowntree and A.C. Pigou. **Lectures on Housing.** Manchester, 1914.

4. C.E.B. Russell. **Social Problems of the North.** London and Oxford, 1913.

5. Henry Solly. **Working Men's Social Clubs and Educational Institutes.** London, 1904.

6. E.J. Urwick, Ed. **Studies of Boy Life in Our Cities.** London, 1904.

7. Alfred Williams. **Life in a Railway Factory.** London, 1915.

8. [Women's Co-operative Guild]. **Maternity. Letters from Working-Women, Collected by the Women's Co-operative Guild with a preface by the Right Hon. Herbert Samuel, M.P.** London, 1915.

9. Women's Co-operative Guild. **Working Women and Divorce. An Account of Evidence Given on Behalf of the Women's Co-operative Guild before the Royal Commission on Divorce.** London, 1911.

    bound with Anna Martin. **The Married Working Woman. A Study.** London, 1911.

M3